Ivan Soden

PLACES

Hopelessness to Happiness

Joe Boyd

Trading PLACES

Hopelessness to Happiness

Joe Boyd

TIMELESS
— PUBLICATIONS —

Timeless Publications Ltd.,
Castlerock,
Northern Ireland.

ISBN 978-1-9993316-6-5

CONTENTS

FOREWORD vii

INTRODUCTION XI

CHAPTER ONE
Twins 15

CHAPTER TWO
'He's Retarded' 19

CHAPTER THREE
Going Places 23

CHAPTER FOUR
'You Will Be a Great Journalist One Day, Joseph' 27

CHAPTER FIVE
God Comes Knocking 33

CHAPTER SIX
'Thank You That Joseph Is with Us' 37

CHAPTER SEVEN
'Legs Out Straight, Joseph' 45

CHAPTER EIGHT
'I Think You Have the Ability to Go to a Normal Secondary School' 49

CHAPTER NINE
'Who on Earth Are You?' 53

CHAPTER TEN
'Joseph Is Slow to Learn' 63

CHAPTER ELEVEN
'He Needs Another Operation' 71

CHAPTER TWELVE
'You Did Really Well' 77

CHAPTER THIRTEEN
'It's Not a School; It's a Training Centre' 81

CHAPTER FOURTEEN
'I Don't Think We Can Help You Here' 91

CHAPTER FIFTEEN
'You Aim Very High, Joe'....................97

CHAPTER SIXTEEN
'We Should Be Encouraging All Students, Whatever Their Need'....................105

CHAPTER SEVENTEEN
Time for a Change....................111

CHAPTER EIGHTEEN
'Would You Like to Stay with Us?'....................119

CHAPTER NINETEEN
'You Have Enormous Potential Academically'....................125

CHAPTER TWENTY
'You're One of Those Paper Boys, Aren't You?'....................135

CHAPTER TWENTY-ONE
'Here's One For You, Joe'....................143

CHAPTER TWENTY-TWO
Shakin' with Embarrassment....................151

CHAPTER TWENTY-THREE
Made in God's Image....................159

CHAPTER TWENTY-FOUR
'I Know Someone You Would Like'....................167

CHAPTER TWENTY-FIVE
'An Incredible Feat'....................179

CHAPTER TWENTY-SIX
'Would You Like to Do Some Writing for Us?'....................187

CHAPTER TWENTY-SEVEN
'We Want to Read Your Story'....................197

CHAPTER TWENTY-EIGHT
'Now It All Makes Sense'....................201

FOREWORD

It has been my privilege and pleasure to know Joe Boyd for the better part of thirty years. In that time, I have grown to admire him immensely. This is neither because of his undoubted courage nor because of his many achievements in the face of difficult odds. The thing which makes Joe who he is and stands out above everything else is his clear, deep, personal faith in the Lord Jesus Christ. It is the Lord who has shaped and moulded Joe's life and enabled him to face many battles with courage and determination. What you are about to read will open your eyes to the variety of struggles, failures, and triumphs Joe has encountered and continues to encounter daily.

Through it all, Joe's primary concern has been that His Saviour should be glorified. His faith has been tested in the crucible of the Lord's will and purposes and has been found genuine. Joe has discovered that genuine faith does not enable one to float through life, smiling at every sorrow. Rather, faith is deepened and strengthened by the Lord's grace as He guides His people through many valleys of tears into a closer walk with Himself.

Joe's great sense of humour enables him to laugh at himself and his problems. I well remember pushing him in his wheelchair through Banbridge and trying to enter a packed coffee shop. I was about to turn away when Joe laughed and said, 'Push me on into it, and watch what happens. Disability has some benefits.' The crowd parted like the waters of the Red Sea before Moses, and folks rushed to make room for a smiling Joe.

However, Joe's life has not been all smiles. A sense of humour carries one only so far, and I have seen Joe cry and have listened to some of his struggles with God's will for his life and future. His honest account of those struggles contained within these pages is a challenge to everyone who reads this book. You will not find a trivial account of a walk with the Lord; rather, you will discover the story of spiritual warfare at an everyday level as you read of the Lord's faithfulness to a weak man. Joe is His child, and God has blessed him in the midst of all kinds of circumstances. It is my hope that you will rejoice in the successes in Joe's life and cry when he struggles. But above all, my prayer is that you will come to know and love the Christ who is carrying him through to the wonders of heavenly glory.

> Blessed be the God and Father of our Lord Jesus Christ! According to his great mercy, he has caused us to be born again to a living hope through the resurrection of Jesus

Christ from the dead, to an inheritance that is imperishable, undefiled, and unfading, kept in heaven for you, who by God's power are being guarded through faith for a salvation ready to be revealed in the last time. In this you rejoice, though now for a little while, if necessary, you have been grieved by various trials, so that the tested genuineness of your faith—more precious than gold that perishes though it is tested by fire—may be found to result in praise and glory and honour at the revelation of Jesus Christ. (1 Peter 1:3–7 ESV)

Rev Brian Boyd

INTRODUCTION

Spastic diplegia is a type of cerebral palsy, which, in my case, was caused by the lack of oxygen available to my brain at birth. (Premature birth can also be a contributory factor, although my twin, Mark, is able-bodied.) *Spastic* describes the spasms or involuntary movements that can impact people with the condition. *Cerebral* refers to the cerebrum, the affected area of the brain. *Palsy* depicts the paralysis that occurs within the muscles of those affected.

No two people who have cerebral palsy are affected in quite the same way. I walk with a noticeable stagger. My fine motor skills are also affected, with the implication that my handwriting resembles that of a three-year-old. I experience stiffness and pain every day, particularly in my legs, back, and knees. Spasms and involuntary body movements also occur, especially when I am tired. My speech is generally okay, except when I am tired and my mouth muscles tighten, causing me to speak with a slur. Family and friends agree that one positive to emerge from this symptom is that I usually stop talking—a blessing they rarely experience at any other time.

Cognitively, I possess a high level of intelligence; however, the part of my brain that controls my coordination as well as my visual and spatial awareness is damaged. This makes crossing busy roads on my own challenging, as I cannot judge the speed and distance of oncoming traffic. For that same reason, driving a car has proved impossible for me. This frustrates me since it limits my independence in human terms. With age, however, I have come to realise that for over forty years, God has enabled me to travel to the places He needs me to be, so I will leave the transport provision to Him. The limitation I struggle with most in this regard is not in getting to concerts, cinema, or holidays but simply the inability to nip to the shops when we run out of milk, razor blades, or chocolate. Perhaps God is protecting my waistline?

Based purely on my own situation, my life mirrors the sentiments expressed by the apostle Paul in 2 Corinthians 12:7–10.

> Therefore, in order to keep me from becoming conceited, I was given a thorn in my flesh, a messenger of Satan, to torment me. Three times I pleaded with the Lord to take it away from me. But he said to me, "My grace is sufficient for you, for my power is made perfect in weakness." Therefore, I will boast all the more gladly about my weaknesses, so that Christ's power may rest on me. That is why, for

> Christ's sake, I delight in weaknesses, in insults, in hardships, in persecutions, in difficulties. For when I am weak, then I am strong.

Applying this to my life, God has enabled me to accomplish amazing things. Medical and other professionals have been astounded by what I have achieved despite my physical disability. I also know that I am prone to complacency and arrogance in so many situations. As I meditate on my frustrations, I realise that the things which hold me back are the very things which keep me dependent on God. All too often, human beings, myself included, receive a blessing from God only to think that we have accomplished it. The result is that we drift away from Him as we celebrate the gift as emanating from our hard work rather than from the overflowing storehouses of Christ's goodness.

My purpose in writing *Trading Places* is threefold. Firstly, I desire to reveal how God has changed my life—the existence of a very ordinary Christian man—for the better. Secondly, I want to take you along on my journey of grace with Him as we delve together into my past life events and talk about my walk alongside Him today. This will, I believe, demonstrate how His grace has been active throughout my life—for my good and the benefit of others and all for His glory. Thirdly, I long to share how God has moved generously and often miraculously to allow me to fulfil my lifelong dream of becoming a journalist and writer even when many people believed this goal was beyond my reach.

My story demonstrates that God is still in the business of accomplishing miracles. I pray that Christians, particularly those who are struggling in their faith or awaiting the fulfilment of a long-term promise from our Creator, may be encouraged to keep believing. Your Saviour has not forgotten His promises to you, and they will come to pass even if the obstacles seem humanly insurmountable.

My wider aspiration for *Trading Place: 'From Insanity to the Saviour'* is that it will speak into the lives of non-Christians by demonstrating that not only is God real but He is infinitely powerful and active. He is not a Santa Claus figure who can be ignored by a sophisticated society. He is Lord of everything and can do amazing things in the lives of those He created. That means everyone. I hope that will become evident as you read this book.

I cannot claim to be a writer in the class of Dickens or Shakespeare, but I have been blessed to see God at work in my life through the best and worst of times. I have a personal relationship with the Saviour, and I know that my Redeemer lives. I feel driven, even compelled, to pen this book because only God could have moved to make possible the events I describe. Any encouragement, blessing, or hope you may glean from this is down to Him.

To God be the glory!

CHAPTER ONE

TWINS

My Place Predestined

The long, hot summer of 1976 was approaching, and a young couple from rural North Antrim was looking forward to their wedding.

Nineteen-year-old Margaret Hannah Elizabeth Maxwell, who had just graduated from Portrush Catering College, was engaged to Stanley Boyd, a dairyman. The middle child of seven, Mum was born on 5 January 1957 to a farming family on the Whitesides Road close to Randalstown. William (Willie) Maxwell and his wife, Agnes, known as Nan to this day, headed the clan.

Just a few years earlier, on 11 April 1953, neighbouring landowners Joseph (Joe) Boyd Sr. and his good lady, Rachael, or Rita, as she was known, welcomed little Stanley into the world. He was fourth in a brood of five children who grew up at Terrygowan.

Mum and Dad met just before her sixteenth birthday at a New Year's Eve shindig, which took place on Maxwell's farm. Very soon, they were an item, and on 21 April 1976, the young lovebirds were married in Brookside Presbyterian Church, Ahoghill, by Rev Ivan McKay, a future Moderator of the Presbyterian Church in Ireland.

Excited at the beginning of their new life together, my parents were keen to start a family as soon as possible and were delighted when Mum fell pregnant just a few months later. Granny, I am told, reacted to this news: 'Spare me this day, you married one minute and pregnant the next!'

By the time Mum's pregnancy was in full bloom, Mum and Dad had moved to Kells, where they lived for a time on the Crosshill View estate. An X-ray confirmed what the local general practitioner Dr Liam Simpson had already suspected. The newlyweds were expecting twins.

What wasn't foreseen, however, was our early arrival, nearly six weeks ahead of the due date. Obviously, I cannot remember anything about my birth, so I will let Mum talk you through those events.

'It was a beautiful day, perfect drying weather, so I had tackled my washing pile. I was feeling fine as I went to bed in the evening only to awaken in the middle of the night as I realised my waters had started to break.

'We didn't have a telephone, and it was before the

time of mobile phones, so we had to go to the phone box in Kells. We rang the Waveney Hospital in Ballymena and were told to come straight in.

'I was just over thirty-three weeks along, so the medical staff gave me injections to try to stop the labour. This proved impossible to do, so I was transferred to the Labour Ward. Joe was arriving head first while Mark was a breach birth. The boys were tangled up, and I had to be put to sleep. It was a normal birth and Dr Liam's brother Hugo delivered the twins.

'Joe arrived first, weighing three pounds nine ounces, followed by Mark, who was four pounds one ounce. Both boys were put straight into an incubator. My first memory of them was watching on as my two babies were rushed to the Special Care Baby Unit at The Royal Victoria Hospital in Belfast.'

Understandably tired, Mum slept for several hours after we were born. By the time she was awake, Dad and Mum's older sister Mary had already named us: Joseph in honour of my grandfather, while my twin brother, Mark, was given the male equivalent of Mum's name (Margaret).

In 1977, premature babies faced an even bigger fight to survive than they do now. Four weeks passed before Mark was allowed home, then weighing five pounds five ounces. I left the hospital one week later, tipping the scales at five pounds two ounces.

No one could tell my parents whether or not we would live. That we had survived the first hard month was surely proof that God had a plan for Mark's life as well as for mine. However, only the Lord knew at that time how events would subsequently unfold. What happened to me would astound my family, the doctors, and other professionals who would work with me in the years ahead.

CHAPTER TWO

'HE'S RETARDED'

Stuck in a Hopeless Place?

Right from the beginning of my life, Mum recalls that I was a bad feeder and that my swallow reflex was poor. More often than not, she says, the contents of my bottle went right back out the way it came in! I was missing my milestones. By the time we were six months old, Mark was sitting up while I was still lying. Whether these things were the result of my yet undiagnosed condition is uncertain; however, Mum's intuition told her that something was wrong.

'Don't worry about him; he's fine,' the health visitor said when Mum queried my slow development. 'You will have to do something about Mark, though. He is too fat!' Mum felt that health care professionals were belittling her concerns about me still further.

As our first birthday approached, Mark was walking, but I had yet to take my first steps. Even then, the health visitors who worked with me did not seem concerned about my lack of progress. Their laissez-faire attitude to my situation came to an abrupt halt around six months later when I was sent to see a consultant paediatrician. The news she delivered to my parents turned their world upside down.

'I am afraid Joseph is retarded.'

To my young parents in late 1978, this diagnosis was devastating. Mum recalls that my dad went home and nearly had a nervous breakdown. He was a young, uneducated man from a rural background who was trying to come to terms with a horrendous situation. Within the context of the then current medical knowledge and societal attitudes, Dad struggled to know what to do with me or expect from me.

Less understandable was the attitude of certain medical practitioners who, perhaps, should have known better, especially in the presence of the child in question. But we were living in a different time. I remember with acute pain the words of one doctor who called to our home to check on my progress. As he worked his way down a checklist, he casually remarked, 'Joseph would be about two years behind his brother then.' Those words rang in my ears for many years and made me question myself regularly. Am I slow? Am I worthy of anyone's time? What's the point in anything I do? I will always be viewed as running behind everyone else, so who cares?

For her part, Mum appeared to cope better with my situation than anyone—a scenario I now realise is not uncommon in parents of a child with a disability. However, her outward appearance disguised the pain only a mother could understand. Mum has been a committed Christian from the age of seventeen, and she once confided in me that she used to pray every morning for a miracle for me—that I would wake up cured.

That did not happen in the sense Mum had originally hoped, but God was about to answer her prayers in an equally amazing way.

CHAPTER THREE

GOING PLACES

A Visitor Comes Calling

In 1979, a young doctor named James Kenny joined Liam Simpson at the surgery in Kells. His arrival proved to be a watershed moment in my life.

Mum recalls, 'The moment Dr Kenny saw you, he immediately recognised the symptoms: spastic diplegia, a form of cerebral palsy. He then referred us to a specialist, who confirmed this diagnosis. He said something about this being the lesser of two evils, but they weren't able to tell us very much.'

The diagnosis of cerebral palsy, which is primarily a physical disability, proved to be game changer for me and my family.

Soon afterwards, Ethel Kenny visited Mum. Ethel was quite simply an angel in human form sent from heaven. She had a son, Stephen, who had been born with spina bifida in the late 1950s, at a time when children with disabilities were viewed as objects of pity at best and shame at worst.

Mrs Kenny used her experience as a mother to change forever the way children with disabilities in Ballymena, and beyond, were viewed. She worked alongside doctors, teachers, politicians, and parents to ensure the best possible opportunities were available to the young people in her care. Her work and insight radically transformed the lives of disabled children by making education and daily physical therapy available to them. On one occasion she refused a request from a major political icon to close her school. She was not afraid to lock horns with prominent and sometimes intimidating public figures.

Ethel was widely respected and admired by those whose paths she crossed. She was warm-hearted and compassionate. One fierce journalist told me. 'I will gladly do anything for Ethel.'

Ethel had a huge impact on my life from the very outset of our meeting, securing my place at a local playgroup for children with spina bifida and other physical disabilities. My parents were delighted. I was less enthusiastic. Apparently, my attempts to avoid playgroup were extreme, though largely futile. Recalling my time there, Mum smiles. 'It was awful. You just hated going and threw up every morning. I was a hard cow and put you on the bus anyway.' Though Mum made me go, every chance I got I tried to escape by running out the playschool door, only to have the head of the playgroup, Lily Hayes, chase me down.

God's timing, however, was perfect. Many of the children

at that playgroup migrated with me to Beechgrove Special School, which opened in Ballymena in late 1980. Ethel Kenny was the driving force behind its opening. She lobbied for a special school when she was part of the spina bifida group in Ballymena. Specialising in working with children with physical disability, Beechgrove was the first school of its kind to be opened outside of Belfast, and Ethel, a teacher by profession, became its founding principal.

Ethel Kenny impacted the lives of countless children with disabilities for the better, including my own. I truly believe that God sent her as His instrument to shape my future.

CHAPTER FOUR

'YOU WILL BE A GREAT JOURNALIST ONE DAY, JOSEPH'

My Place Foretold

It is difficult to overestimate the influence Ethel Kenny had on my life. This is true from the time I was a toddler right up until her death in 2002. I knew her as a middle-aged woman with a healthy mane of blonde hair. Her voice sounded more like a mum than a headmistress. She had a mother's heart to match. More clichés, like *a gifted teacher*, *inspiring*, and *dedicated*, could be penned to describe her, yet they fall far short of adequately expressing the woman she was. Mum sums it well: 'From the moment you met Ethel, you couldn't help but love her.'

Mrs. Kenny knew each of her pupils and their

families by name and was aware of the individual circumstances of each situation. She knew intimate details of many, yet she never divulged personal information. She took time to really know and understand those in her care, and, consequently, she knew exactly how best to help them. Her influence extended above and beyond what anyone might have expected. Sometime after I left Beechgrove, when I was waiting for my lift to the Rotary Club Camp for Disabled Boys, an event which was run by the Belfast branch of this organisation, my escort had failed to show up. Mum wondered what to do and decided to ring Mrs. Kenny. Ten minutes later, the president of Ballymena Rotary Club was at my front door in his shiny Mercedes to drive me all the way from Kells in County Antrim to Crawfordsburn in County Down.

Quite simply, Ethel Kenny did all she could to help those she loved, and her pupils knew it. Her experiences as a mother of a child with a physical disability had left her neither bitter nor fearful; instead, the adversity fortified this remarkable lady with a determination to change the world for her son, Stephen, and many, many others. She founded Beechgrove and instigated the building of the Northern Ireland Council for Orthopaedic Development (NICOD) Training Centre, which I would later join. Ethel was a loving yet fearless woman. When asked by future First Minister Ian Paisley to close Beechgrove during the Ulster Says NO protests, her reply was, 'We will not be closing;

we are a special school.'

Her mantra to her pupils was always very simple: 'Don't focus on the things you can't do; think about the things you can do.'

When it became apparent that my ability to physically write would elude me, Mrs Kenny brought a Brother typewriter out of the school store. This simple but practical idea set me on a path that would lead me to write for *Ballymena Times*, the *Belfast Telegraph*, the *Newsletter*, and The Church Page, not to mention writing this book and two others.

As I learned to express my thoughts by typing, it quickly became apparent to my headmistress that I was 'good at constructing sentences.' At a Parents' Evening, she told Mum that my grasp of the English language was 'extraordinary'. I was a keen reader, and I quickly developed the ability to compose stories. By the time I was eight years old, I had begun to listen to the news and compile what I called my School Teletext Service, a regurgitation of the news bulletin I had heard on the early breakfast TV each morning. I would type it out on the School's BBC Mirco computer then read it to my classmates before lunch. They listened kindly, but I am sure some of them must have thought it strange that I relished every opportunity to write and report on current events.

As a boy with a disability, I had often felt different from other children and, to a certain extent, inferior to them; so I loved finally being able to excel at something. I couldn't run as fast or operate my hands as well as many of my peers, and I was always last to be picked for any physical team games. I knew my physical limitations, yet writing stories was a completely different ball game. Here was something I could do as well as, if not better than, anyone. My condition did not limit my ability to write. I was special, and I stood out from the others, but this time it was for all the right reasons.

Even now when I am in pain, I find that composing an article or two is more soothing than any painkiller I could swallow. Many of the articles I have written over the years were penned or typed from my bed or comfy sofa when I experienced too much pain to leave the house. No one has ever forced me to work when I am not feeling well; indeed, my employers have discouraged it and ordered me to rest. Often I have ignored them, sometimes to my detriment, but my writing provides a means of escape from what can be a depressing and agonising physical condition. With laptop at hand, it is just me, the real me, who inhabits my soul. That person is accompanied only by the English language and my readers. The gift of writing that God has given me transcends any physical disability. I will be forever grateful to the Lord for blessing me in this way.

For her part, Mrs Kenny was thrilled by my progress and arranged for a short article highlighting my endeavours to be featured in the *Ballymena Guardian*. I wrote a piece telling the readers about myself and revealing that I liked to 'write books and stories' using the school computer, while Mrs. Kenny waxed lyrically about what a 'bright boy' I was and how much the computer had helped me and others like me who physically struggled to handwrite our thoughts.

From then on, my proud teacher entered me in writing competitions, and I did enjoy some success. While at Beechgrove, I won a book as a token in a contest organised by Ballymena Central Library.

Even before that, Mrs Kenny told me, 'You will be a great journalist one day, Joseph.' She lived long enough to see me join the *Ballymena Times* and was one of the first people I interviewed as a cub reporter there. Her final recorded words to me on the Dictaphone were: 'Joe, I just want to say that I am very proud to be one of your first victims. I am glad to have been your teacher. I am very proud of you.' I will never forget these precious words and the dear lady who uttered them. She gave me a strong sense of destiny, which remains with me to this day. It no longer mattered that others uttered negative forecasts regarding my future, I knew in my heart that I was better than my circumstances. Ethel Kenny, the most wonderful Christian lady I have met, instilled in me her belief, and I am so thankful that God used her to show me the way.

CHAPTER FIVE

GOD COMES KNOCKING

The Best Place Assured

Whether at Beechgrove or closer to home, I was surrounded by a great deal of genuine and loving Christian influence as a child. Mum came to faith at the age of seventeen, thanks largely to the faithful witness and prayers of her godly aunt Hannah, who also devoted her life to caring for her mentally disabled younger brother, Hugh.

Mum would fondly tell my brother Mark and me of how Aunt Hannah took her and her siblings to Brookside Presbyterian Church in Ahoghill every Sunday. Keen that her nieces and nephews should have a good understanding of the Sacraments, Hannah encouraged them to stay in church during Communion rather leave for the children's activities.

Hannah's intercessions were answered, and Mum

insisted that I, along with Mark and our younger sister, Megan, would grow up in the church and attend all the programmes appropriate for our ages. I must confess that many times I protested about going; however, looking back, I am grateful for those years. In fact, I would go as far as to say that thanks largely to Mum's determination and good teaching in my formative years, I don't ever remember a time when I didn't know that God loved me and that I needed to accept His Son, Jesus, as my personal Saviour.

When Mark and I were about six or seven years old, we attended a Sunday school class in Kells Presbyterian Church. Our two teachers, Margaret Kernohan and Amanda McCullough, told our class that to be saved, we needed to 'ask Jesus to come into your heart and shut the door'. If we prayed that prayer and really meant it, we were assured that Jesus would gladly become our Saviour and be our friend in this life before taking us to heaven at the right time.

Very soon afterwards, Mark and I talked about what we had heard in Sunday school, and we both got down on our knobbly knees in the bedroom we shared and prayed, 'Dear God, I am sorry for all of the bad things I have done. Please take away my sins and come into my heart and shut the door. Amen.'

Looking back, it was a simple, child-like prayer, but both of us sincerely meant it. I do believe that my brother and I were saved at that moment. Speaking for myself, many times since then I had not walked as closely with God as I should, and I am grateful for His promise in 2 Timothy 2:13: 'If we are faithless, He remains faithful, for He cannot deny Himself' (NASB). Another verse that challenges and comforts me is from Deuteronomy 7:9, 'Know therefore that the LORD your God is God, the faithful God who keeps His covenant and steadfast love with those who love Him and keep His commands, to a thousand generations' (ESV). Awesome promises indeed, they have kept me in the faith well through my primary school years and beyond.

Even as a young child I was keen to tell everyone that I was a Christian and that they needed to be saved. One of the physiotherapists from Beechgrove remembered me as 'The little boy who knew every song Rev William McCrea ever recorded.'

The Lord also blessed me with many of his wonderful servants who willingly nurtured my young faith.

CHAPTER SIX

'THANK YOU THAT JOSEPH IS WITH US'

Finding My Place in the World

In Kells Presbyterian Church, I could not have had a better spiritual home. Margaret and Amanda's very simple lesson on 'asking Jesus into your heart', which prompted me to become a Christian, was the culmination of years of great teaching and Christian care.

I enjoyed attending the Christian Endeavour every Friday night. Greta Maybin, an elderly local farmer's wife, Pat Swann, a secondary school teacher, and Mary Elliott, who worked in the local branch of Woolworths, ran the younger section of this organisation. These were ordinary women yet true saints of God. They didn't just preach the Word, they lived it, and their warm and loving dispositions made

Christianity attractive. If this is what Christians were, then I wanted to please them and grow up to be like them.

A middle-aged couple, Alex and Thelma Meneely, was very good to Mark and me when we were children. They often had us round to their house for tea and the occasional game of snooker. They were always patient, with a gentle manner and sincere faith characterising their lives. Even though they are both now in heaven, I can clearly recall their faces and voices—a testament to their lasting impact on my young life. Another husband and wife duo, Jimmy and Edna Mawhinney, who sat beside us in church, also showed kindness and love to our family, both inside and outside the fellowship.

The same was true of the officers of the 1st Connor Boys' Brigade Company (BB), which was based at the nearby Connor Presbyterian Church. Pearl Picken, Anne Agnew, and the leader-in-charge, Lynn McBurney, directed the Robins, as they were then known. When I was about six years old, I returned to BB after my first round of surgery. Lynn opened the meeting in prayer: 'Lord, we thank you that Joseph is back at Robins tonight after his operation, and we pray that he will be with us every night from now on. . . .' I was humbled that a grown-up thought I was important enough to be prayed for out loud in church.

Another Robins leader who holds a very special place in my heart was a young woman called Angela Barr (later McCartney). Angela was a beautifully generous person, and she made it her business to ensure that I was fully involved in all the activities. She became my legs during games and codesigned my art projects. More than that, Angela believed in me, and she wasn't afraid to make her feelings known if she sensed that I was being sidelined by anyone else.

Many years later when I received my Queens' Badge (the highest award a young man can achieve in the BB) and was about to be appointed to the rank of Staff Sergeant, Angela was there. 'You've got your Queen's Badge, and you are going to be an officer. I always said you could do it,' she said.

***

I was a proud member of Fernisky Junior Orange Lodge as a child and a teenager. I loved being part of this because, from the very moment I joined, my disability was never a problem. I was encouraged to travel the length of the province, competing in quizzes and football matches with the other boys. We went on holidays to Donaghadee, and there was never a question of my not going because I was disabled.

Competing in those quizzes against boys from up and down the country and across the water taught me how to win and lose in the real world. In special schools, tiniest achievements are often made to seem greater than they are. This is not necessarily a bad thing for those children who truly struggle to attain anything outside of school. However, when a well-meaning but misguided professional applauds to the rafters an intelligent child with a physical disability for spelling his or her name correctly, a helpful life-lesson is missed. When I won those quizzes as part of an able-bodied team, I learned how it felt to succeed and win genuine peer approval. When we lost, I learned to accept it, shake hands with the victor, and move on. We couldn't avoid the fact that, at times, everyone falls short of their intended goal.

As part of the Junior Orange Order, I learned to respect people from other traditions. We were taught history from a Protestant perspective, but never once were we encouraged to denigrate those of a different religious persuasion. One occasion, as we were coming home from a competition, we passed a lady called Kathleen, whom we knew to be a Catholic. The superintendent of our Lodge, Jim Rodgers, waved to her and said, 'Do you know something, boys? She is the nicest woman you will ever meet. She plays the accordion all over the country. I have heard her at meetings for the Grand Lodge of Ireland.'

We learned from an early age that sectarian bigotry was not acceptable.

***

It goes without saying that Beechgrove School and its staff played a key role in helping me to find my place in the world. The school unashamedly created a Christian atmosphere, which started with Mrs Kenny and flowed from her. Most of the teachers, classroom assistants, and therapists were Christian girls, and they didn't hide that fact. Girls like Anna-May Carson, Annabelle Millar, Ruth Calderwood, and others showed what it meant to live and work as Jesus intended. They could be firm with us out of necessity, but we always knew they loved us. Their attitude and witness had a profound effect on me. I hope I model their love and care as I carry out my work with youth and children.

Their care went hand in hand with a determination to ensure that we received the best possible education. They expected us to turn in our homework on time, and I spent more than a few lunchtimes on detention for deliberately failing to complete weekend assignments by Monday. At one point I dared to complain to one of the teachers, Mrs. Cameron, about 'not being a fan of dictionary work'. 'Well, you will have to make yourself a fan of it,' was her reply.

Similarly, physio and occupational therapists expected me to do my best, work hard, and appreciate the opportunities I had been given. One time, when I was being taught to ride a tricycle as part of my Occupational Therapy, I climbed onto the equipment and was being careless and immature, zigzagging from side to side on the road and not watching out for traffic. The therapist said, 'Joseph, you are like a manic on that bike. You won't get to keep it if you don't use it properly.' I was annoyed, but she was, of course, right.

Bad behaviour at Beechgrove would land the wrongdoer in a spell in 'the punishment chair'. If that weren't bad enough, the parents would receive a phone call letting them know what had happened.

When I arrived home after sitting in the punishment chair, my father's scowl indicated his anger. 'Joseph, why were you in the punishment chair today?' When I owned up to my crime, my father punished me. Of course, I didn't enjoy this at the time or the enforcement of homework. Between Beechgrove and my parents making sure that owned up to and paid the price for my misdeeds, I clearly learned right from wrong. My classmates and I were not brought up with a sense of entitlement simply because we had a disability.

As is true of most young children, my friends were an important part of those early years. One of my first friends and classmates in nursery school at Beechgrove was a little boy named Russell Calderwood. Russell had a big mop of curly black hair, big eyes, and a most infectious giggle. His disability made it difficult for him to move, so he spent most days perched on a large beanbag cushion as he watched the world around him.

I loved making Russell laugh. One afternoon I went down the slide at the corner of our classroom on my tummy, something that young Master Calderwood found hilarious. 'Joseph, stop going down the slide on your tummy.' He giggled helplessly. His pleas had no effect; the more he giggled, the more determined I was to slide on my belly.

Another friend, Jonathan Boyd (no relation), had a form of cerebral palsy so severe that he couldn't walk, talk, or do anything for himself. Yet everyone loved

Jonathan and stopped by his desk to talk to him each day.

One Friday Mrs. Kenny announced that Patrick Morrison, a very shy five-year-old, would join our class at the beginning of the following week. 'I want you all to get to know Patrick. He told his daddy that he was worried about having no friends.' Come Monday, the whole school made a beeline for Patrick, determined to make sure he had plenty of friends!

Sadly, Russell, Jonathan, and Patrick are no longer with us. Russell and Patrick passed away as young children, and Jonathan was only twenty-five when he left this earth. I mention these three boys because through them I learned that human life is fragile and that life is for living. For me, doing anything other than exactly what I want to do or believe I am called to do is never a waste of time or effort.

Thankfully, many of my school friends are still here, and we enjoyed many happy years together, particularly at Beechgrove, where we were given weekly lessons in swimming at the local leisure centre and went horseback riding at the Ballymena branch of Riding for the Disabled. What a lovely childhood! Special schools provide their pupils with many wonderful extra-curricular activities that their able-bodied peers do not get to experience. Often, these are enriching and highpoint experiences in difficult lives, especially for those children whose lives are short-lived or for those who endure painful surgeries.

In comparison with many other of my schoolmates,

I was blessed to undergo only three major operations, two in childhood and another during adolescence, each presenting challenges for myself and my family. I must confess that at the time of these procedures, I did not consider myself very fortunate. I hated having to go away and stay in a hospital thirty miles from home where I knew I would be sore and away from my family and friends. I was not an especially brave sufferer either. I frequently cried with distress or pain when asked to move or exercise after surgery. It is only with the benefit of hindsight that I have realised I was given an easier ride that some of my peers who endured ten or fifteen surgeries necessitating months, not weeks, in hospital.

CHAPTER SEVEN

'LEGS OUT STRAIGHT, JOSEPH'

Getting My Limbs in the Right Place

My first round of surgery was performed at Musgrave Park Hospital in Belfast when I was four or five years old. Its purpose was to lengthen my hamstrings and reduce the tightness in flexion (bend) in my knees and legs. The outcome would ensure that walking and standing would be more comfortable. I am happy to say that it worked.

The second of my childhood operations, which was also relatively successful, involved the straightening of my feet. Able-bodied feet and toes point forward in a straight fashion. Often, the feet of children who have cerebral palsy and similar conditions are curled outwards. As a result, walking is difficult, painful, and even dangerous because it is hard to maintain one's balance.

My memories of these early surgeries are hazy because I was so young. I do recall being in pain and crying. I felt sick because I did not like soggy breakfast cereal. So terrified was I by the noise of the electric machine the doctors used to remove my post-op cast that I wept bitterly until they agreed to stop and use scissors.

Mum did not drive in those days, but, God bless her, she managed to make her way up to Belfast every day to visit me, sometimes more than once, often staying long into the night and occasionally remaining overnight at my side.

Recently, I asked her what she remembered about life during those two hospital procedures and immediately her eyes lit up. 'Our house in Glenaan Park only had a very small toilet, and it was a nightmare getting you in and out of the bathroom, but we managed. Once you were out of plaster, you loved to sit with your knees bent—your father and I use to speak in unison: "Legs out straight, Joseph." Much to your annoyance.'

According to Mum, getting me back on my feet was a real struggle, until she and physiotherapists latched on to an unconventional form of rehabilitation. Not being the most mobile of children, I spent most of my time indoors, and I developed a real love of pop music. At that time Shakin' Stevens was king of the charts. I adored Shaky, and if he advocated something then I wanted it, be it armbands, T-shirts, books, posters, or records, I collected it all.

Armed with this knowledge of my adoration for the 'Welsh Elvis', someone hit on the idea of getting me to dance up and down the parallel bars to Shakin' Stevens. The plan worked, and I took my first steps to the strains of his number one hit, 'This Ole House'.

Years later, I had the opportunity to meet and interview Shaky while I was working for the *Ballymena Times*. I wasted no time in telling him how his music had improved my mobility. He said, 'Thanks for telling me about your walking. I am really pleased to have been a part of that.'

Following each of these first two operations, I was back to Beechgrove, which had a fully operational Physio and Occupational Therapy Department. Susan Pearson, Paddy Ballie, and Joan Bonnar were very patient and gifted practitioners who served many years in the school. I had a real soft spot for Susan, and I have kept in contact with her over the years. I asked her to relate some of the exercises we would have done at that time.

'The exercises were stretches for all your tight muscles, namely your hamstrings, Achilles tendons, and hip extensor. The aim being to prevent contracture. We also did muscle-strengthening work, which included making aeroplanes. This involved lying on your tummy and lifting up your chest. There were push-ups on blocks, using your arms to lift your bottom. I got you to do pull along bench exercises to strengthen your arms.

'Balancing work began on what we call a wobble

board, and we played games such as What Time Is It, Mr Wolf? for balance, start stops, and proper steps. Another one was Froggie, Froggie, May I Cross Your Coloured Water? This was intended to help your standing balance and proper steps. Finally, there was your favourite, 123 Red Lights, to improve your balance and stop-starts.'

Difficult and painful as these exercises sometimes were, Susan and the other therapists worked hard to made them as enjoyable as possible. Beechgrove was an idyllic place where love and acceptance were given freely. Very soon, though, I was to discover that not everywhere was as loving and tolerant. Painful changes lay ahead.

CHAPTER EIGHT

'I THINK YOU HAVE THE ABILITY TO GO TO A NORMAL SECONDARY SCHOOL'

Searching for a New Place

Unlike many other special schools, Beechgrove did not cater to post-primary age children. Consequently, we needed to find another place to continue my education in 1989 when I was about to turn twelve.

Ethel Kenny passionately believed in the benefits of placing children with physical disabilities in mainstream school when it was possible and practical to do so. She saw to it that a good number of my contemporaries were released into mainstream education partway through their time at Beechgrove.

I, however, presented her with a perplexing dilemma, of which I was not fully aware until the opportunity arose for me to talk candidly with her in her later years. I was privileged to spend time with her, which helped me understand why I went down the educational path I did.

During one of our chats, she said, 'I had many a sleepless night over what to do about you, Joe. You were academically capable of going to mainstream school, but you couldn't have coped with it emotionally.'

She was right. The educational psychologist who assessed me in my final year at Beechgrove agreed that I was 'academically capable'. In conjunction with other professionals, her role was to decide where I should go for my post-primary education. I cannot remember much about our time together during which she evaluated me; however, I do recall her asking me, 'Where would you like to go to when you finish here?'

I talked about Fleming Fulton, a large special school in Belfast that had attracted a lot of media attention as a centre of excellence for children and young people with physical disabilities. Pupils there were filmed learning to drive and doing what seemed like advanced work. They looked and sounded as if they enjoyed being there.

The educational psychologist studied me for a moment before saying, 'Are you sure, Joseph? I think you have the ability to go to a normal secondary school.' She was asking me to consider going to a mainstream school, and by affirming my intelligence, she was indicating that it was a possibility.

My reply centred on what I had heard about Fleming Fulton and all the things I thought I could do there.

She closed her notepad. 'Okay, fine. We will take your wishes into consideration when making our decision.'

I had never really considered it could be possible for me to go to a mainstream school. It wasn't something my parents or teachers discussed with me at the time. I was always told that I was at a special school because I was 'handicapped', so I grew to accept that assessment without question. I may have experienced the odd fleeting thought of going to a 'normal' school when a few of my Beechgrove friends transferred to one, but these notions were infrequent. I was happy within my school surroundings, and I assumed that all the other special schools were just as warm and welcoming as Beechgrove. Therefore, my overriding reaction to the educational psychologist's words was a mixture of surprise and, to a certain degree, fear, as I didn't want to go into a mainstream environment that seemed scary and inaccessible to me.

I expected to be going to either Fleming Fulton or Mitchell House, a small, less well-known special school located in our provincial capital city.

During one of our conversations we had years later, Mrs. Kenny told me that she had worried about my ability to fit in at Fleming Fulton because the pupils there were more worldly and less forgiving of those they perceived as teacher's pets. In hindsight, her concerns were valid, although I couldn't have known that at the time. In all honesty, her decision not to place me in mainstream was a sensible one. I was a nervous, easily-made-to-cry, churchgoing child who talked about Sunday school, my minister, and my granny. I often sided with the teacher when my Beechgrove classmates misbehaved and required punishment, though not out of any sense of malice towards them. I simply had a very clear view of right and wrong, and that I was doing the right thing when pulling up my peers for bad behaviour. I was socially naïve in that sense, and because my classmates are Beechgrove were fundamentally good kids who were taught to love one another, they did not seek revenge on me because of my tendency to be a Goody-Two-Shoes. Unfortunately, this would not always be the case in other schools, as I was soon to discover.

CHAPTER NINE

'WHO ON EARTH ARE YOU?'

Choosing the Wrong Place

I have a confession to make. Quite simply, these next few chapters were very challenging to write. They recount some of the most difficult years of my life. Some of the situations I describe were, at least in part, a result of my decisions regarding what school I attended. My behaviour, both at school and at home, affected how others treated me. What lies ahead provides a clear demonstration of God's patience, forgiveness, and ability to restore a person to where He needs them to be, even when they let Him down. Admissions out of the way, let's carry on.

Towards the end of our last term at school, I, along with two other boys who were also leaving Beechgrove, travelled to Belfast with our parents to visit both special schools for pupils with physical disabilities. Mitchell House was a small and very homely place, where pupils were taught in an old building. The elderly headmaster had been there for many years and was friendly enough. However, he lost brownie points for his attitude when one of the parents asked him, 'What exams will the children take before they leave here?' His reply went something like, 'In our school, the pupils we see tend to be in the lower range of academic ability. They are happy, though. We do what we can in our nice environment. Anybody who is academic wouldn't be here.'

By contrast, Fleming Fulton was situated in a wealthy suburb of South Belfast. It boasted a large modern wing that had been built just a few years earlier and was full of special resources. At least two major television documentaries had been made about the complex, each with pupils happy to talk about how much they had achieved while attending school there.

Mind you, the early signs weren't promising. We arrived at the Fleming Fulton and headed for the reception where we were met by one of the office staff who told us to wait while she found someone to show us round. After a good few minutes, a balding, bearded, middle-aged man appeared. 'Who the on earth are you?' he asked.

One of the parents explained that we were there to see around both special schools in Belfast in preparation for we three boys transferring to one of them the next term. The man introduced himself as a Deputy Head and began to lead us round Fleming.

He first showed us the school's swimming pool and the well-equipped PE and music departments. Afterwards, the vice principal took us to the Home Economics room, where we heard the teacher berate a pupil for not putting an eggshell in the bin.

As we trooped slowly round the school, the Deputy Head told our parents about the various external examinations the pupils were given the opportunity to undertake. At that point, my ears pricked up. *Wow. He is talking about kids like me taking GCSEs and getting other big qualifications. If I stay until I am eighteen, I will be sorted. I can go places here.*

When my friends and I went back to Beechgrove the following day, Mrs. Kenny was keen to learn how we had got on during the visits. One of the other lads said, 'I don't want to go to that Fleming Fulton; the teacher told off a boy for dropping an eggshell on the floor.' The other lad chipped, 'Yeah, and the teacher at Fleming Fulton didn't even know we were coming; he looked at us and said, "Who on earth are you?" I want to go to Mitchell House.'

I, on the other hand, said that I *was* impressed by the swimming pool and large PE hall at Fleming Fulton. I talked about doing exams and getting qualifications. I wanted to go to Fleming.

It might seem odd that at age eleven I was thinking about exams and other adult things, but having spent those eleven years trying to prove that I was as capable as my able-bodied peers, I relished the opportunity to show others that I was 'normal'.

Mrs. Kenny and others in Beechgrove confirmed that I was a clever boy and that I could do very well if I worked hard. I determined early on that I wanted to be a newspaper reporter and an author, goals that required me to work hard and pass exams. Talk from Fleming Fulton about doing General Certificate in Secondary Educations (GCSE) and learning to drive only served to stoke my ambitions further.

The powers that be decided that my future lay at Fleming, which excited me. So I said good-bye to Beechgrove as I walked out of its front door for the last time in June 1989.

Ever keen to excel, I innocently asked Mrs. Kenny if I could earn degrees at my new school. No doubt trying to keep me in a positive frame of mind, she said that although I couldn't get one at that school, if I worked hard and did well on the exams, I could go to university afterwards.

One night shortly before Mark and I started our respective P7 years, Dad came into our bedroom and expressed his high hopes for my brother. 'You know, Mark, this is going to be a big year for you. You are going to have to work hard. Some nights you will have to miss the BB, the Lodge, and whatever else, but that's how it is.' Turning to me, he said, 'This year makes little odds. You will be going to one of the special schools whatever happens. So don't worry about it.'

I don't believe Dad meant me any harm. In fact, his words were, to some extent, true. But they did hurt. I wanted to be as accepted in his eyes as Mark was. Therefore, I believed I needed to succeed in the same ways as Mark.

With my head full of aspirations, off I went to the big, impressive school. I felt as nervous as a newborn kitten that first morning. In truth, I wanted to return to my beloved Beechgrove, Mrs. Kenny, and my friends. There was no going back, however; change was happening. I must have talked incessantly to the taxi driver all the way to school, trying to impress him, and feverishly attempting to take my mind off what lay ahead.

Other children who attended a school for the deaf on the Falls Road were also in the taxi: Ruari, Natasha, and Angela. When they introduced themselves to me, I was as polite as I could be, smiling and greeting them, but I was absorbed in my own world. Eventually, the taxi pulled up at Fleming Fulton. The driver hopped out and went to find someone to take me to my classroom.

Eventually, he returned with a tall middle-aged lady. She was friendly and introduced herself as one of the child-care staff, a group of people whose job was to look after the physical needs of each class. She asked, 'Do you want a wheelchair? It is quite a long way from here to your form teacher's room.'

I shook my head. 'No, thank you. I can walk.'

As we made our way around the building, I stared wide-eyed at what seemed like a massive institution, full of corridors and rooms. Beechgrove was a tiny place with two classrooms and one main corridor. I worried I would get lost.

'There are the head-boy and head-girl coming,' my escort said as we approached two tall students.

I smiled. 'Hello.'

They did likewise.

After what seemed like ages, but was probably only a few minutes, we arrived at the music rooms where my form teacher was based. The lady who had met me at the door introduced me to the teacher. I sat down with the other students, who had formed a circle. Everyone was quiet, obviously nervous. Around half of my new classmates had been through the school's primary department, while the remainder, like myself, had transferred from other pre-secondary schools around the province.

Our form teacher had greyish-blonde hair. A friendly woman in her late forties, she had a passion for music, which played a big part in the life of the school. I tried to be enthusiastic by crooning a line of a sitcom theme when she asked me 'Do you sing?' My classmates laughed nervously, thinking, 'What is this guy on?' I know this to be true because a little while later, one of them said, 'Do you remember on the first morning, we were talking about music and he just started to sing?' He then revealed what they had been thinking.

A pupil who had been through the primary department was asked to keep an eye on me for the day, but I lost track of her as soon we left our form room. I followed the others at a distance but was, to be truthful, in a daze.

Some lads were kicking an indoor football around in the corridor. 'Wanna play football, mate?' Clearly, it was not a true invitation to play. He ran the ball across my path, and with a turn reminiscent of George Best, he swerved around me with his crutches, regained control of the ball, and carried on.

I wandered over to a set of red benches behind the cloakroom and caught my breath. I looked around and spotted a large mural of a beach holiday scene adorning the wall of the main corridor. Have A Nice Day was painted along the top.

My first day there was a Friday. Our first-year Friday classes included music, craft, design, technology. I looked forward to Fridays in Form One because the subjects were lighter and more fun—and rarely entailed any homework.

Arriving home from the first day at Fleming Fulton I was exhausted. Mark had just started at a local grammar school that same day. Of course, Mum was full of questions for Mark and me, but neither of us was particularly keen to answer, each of us lost in our own thoughts. Exasperated by our unwillingness to talk, Mum remarked, 'You won't find the answer staring out the window!'

This first year at my secondary school started out well enough, but towards the end of the first year, problems piled up. I began showing the signs of stress expected of a primary one pupil. I had always been a nervous child, even at Beechgrove. I feared failure; I was scared of getting into trouble; and I was anxious to please people, especially adults. When I started to feel the pressure of school, I became unhappy, and these fears and anxieties increased tenfold. I began having 'accidents' wetting myself. I started crying for no apparent reason. My teachers told my parents that I was anxious all the time. When Mum and Dad asked me what I was anxious about, my reply was either a sullen 'Nothing', or I gave a tirade of abuse about something unrelated to deflect attention from their questions.

My unhappiness stemmed from my never feeling accepted in Belfast, either by my fellow pupils or, to a certain degree, by the teachers. Some of that was down to me. I wanted my school in Belfast to be a continuation of the experience I enjoyed at Beechgrove. Quite simply, it was not, and I was naïve and unrealistic to expect that it could be. My classmates were different not only from me but also from my former mates at Beechgrove. They were streetwise, lived in the city, and were uninterested in God, BB, Kells Church, and Shakin' Stevens.

I enjoyed my lessons and was keen in class, but it seemed to me that they just wanted to mess about. They played upon the kinder teachers, and I was quick to tell them it wasn't right. This was not the best way to win friends and influence people, but I was brought up to know right from wrong and saw things as black and white. I'd say things like 'That person at the front of the class is all right' or 'You guys are being stupid. Stop it!' I was, and am, the type of person who enjoys his victories.

If a teacher read out the exam results and I had come out on top, I couldn't help smiling, which only antagonised my peers. They didn't understand that I was smiling with pride and happiness at my achievements not at their failings. I was young and I probably never stopped to consider how my actions got their backs up.

Whatever the rights and wrongs of the scenario were, I became deeply miserable with life at school and at home. Unfortunately, the situation would worsen before it got better.

CHAPTER TEN

'JOSEPH IS SLOW TO LEARN'

A Very Dark Place

By the end of my second year and the start of my third year, school was becoming unbearable for me. I was topping the class in exams, but that was not a particularly great achievement, given that I didn't need to perform anywhere near my best to compete with the rest of my class. In my eyes, they were more interested in bullying softer teachers or pupils and telling crude jokes than being concerned about their results.

Daily some of the other boys asked me questions of a personal and often sexual nature. Being a wet-behind-the-ears, churchgoing, country boy, I didn't at first know what some of these terms meant, so when I asked, 'What's that mean?' They answered with derisive laughter and mockery. I felt like I was from a different world than those boys, one that I had no ability or desire to be a part of.

I became annoyed when one of the better teachers tried to conduct a good lesson, only to be laughed down by these idiots. The rest of the class suffered because of their immaturity. The teachers did tell them off, but in most cases, it seemed like the students thrived on the extra attention and sought to humiliate and frustrate the teacher further, especially if they saw him or her beginning to wilt under a torrent of verbal pressure. The lads I knew from Kells, BB, or the Lodge weren't like these classmates. Though not all of them were Christians, and they might utter an occasional obscenity, they never used this language to deliberately cause offence or to make fun of anyone.

With the guys at school, however, they could be vicious, cruel, and disrespectful. I didn't like most of them. They despised me, whom they referred to as a snob and a queer because I enjoyed my lessons, was polite to the teachers, and came to school with the intention of getting good marks.

Worse still, the attitude from the leaders of the school indicated that they believed I had created the problem by 'failing to integrate with my peers'. One senior teacher suggested that I had set myself up at a target by being different. When my mum went up to school to demand that the administrators do something about my getting picked on, the same deputy head who had first shown us around the school on visiting day told her, 'Joseph is too nicey-nicey, and they don't like that up here. Nobody wants a know-it-all. Maybe he needs to stop putting his hand up in class and answering questions.'

His more articulate colleague, the vice principal in

charge of pastoral care, summoned me to her office and enquired as to why I was a loner who didn't seem to want any friends. She went on to explain how it can be difficult for other pupils to cope with someone they perceive as overconfident.

As I sat in her office, thoughts rolled around in my head. *How on earth can I integrate with people who despise me? Why would I want to be their friend? They chase me up and down the corridors, shouting horrible things they want to inflict upon me while threatening to write a petition to get me out of 'their' school. These kids bully children with severe learning difficulties. Even among themselves, they joke about their mothers being 'ladies of the night.' Surely, the whole point of a teacher asking a question is for someone to answer.*

Hindsight is a wonderful thing, but I wish I had voiced those thoughts to ring in ears of Fleming Fulton's two vice-principals. Venting to them may have prevented me from taking my frustrations out on the people I loved at home.

I used to get mad at Mum and hit her when she asked me to do something. I shouted at her and grabbed her, deliberately causing her pain. I kicked, screamed, shouted, and swore at my brother, my sister, my mother, and my father. No curse word was strong enough, no action wicked enough. I was nasty, twisted, and determined to be as horrid as possible. Dad responded, as most fathers would, with ever more severe physical punishments. His reaction was understandable in the circumstances. Mark said, 'If you punch me, I will punch you harder four times.' And he did.

I have absolutely no excuse for the way I treated my

family, especially Mum. I am truly 100 percent sorry for the pain, physical and emotional, I caused that lovely woman. I have asked her forgiveness many times, to which she says, 'You have nothing to be sorry for. Your sins are washed away in God's sea of forgetfulness to be remembered no more.' Mum and I are now exceptionally close, and this is much more than I deserve. She is a picture of God's grace.

One of the many actions that still haunt me from that time involves my dear grandfather. Mum sent Mark, Megan, me over to see our grandparents one Monday afternoon during the school holidays. I had protested all morning that I didn't want to go but wasn't given a choice. When it came time to return home, I bolted out of my grandparents' door towards the car. As I was leaving, Granda said, 'Bye, Joseph. I will see you sometime again.'

I barely grunted my response. 'Aye, Granda, bye.' I didn't even stop to look at him properly. On Friday of that week, Granda collapsed in his garden from a massive heart attack, which killed him instantly. He was gone, just sixty-six years old. The grandson whom he carried up and down the beach as a child ignored the last opportunity to speak to him. What a complete and utter idiot I was. A selfish little fool.

My behaviour at home was made more inexcusable because, even at my cruellest, I could still turn on the charm when I wanted to impress people. I was a Non-Commissioned Officer at Boys Brigade and a Chaplain in the Junior Orange Order. I loved these activities, as well as the Christian Endeavour, where I spoke regularly. Mum often threatened to tell the church members about my behaviour. I have no doubt that she confided in some—she needed to and deserved to—however, I did not receive the humiliation or demotions I deserved. By maintaining her silence, Mum showed a picture of mercy! Who can understand the depth or purposes of God's mercy and grace? Isn't it (He) amazing????

At the time, I believed I had valid reasons for my behaviour—though it seems ridiculous in retrospect. I was expressing my frustration in the one place I thought I could get away with it: at home. At the special school, we were always told not to hit fellow pupils in case they had a hidden disability, which being thumped could cause them to become ill or worse. I was proud of my achievements at church, BB, and the Lodge and didn't want to jeopardise these by misbehaving there. Fundamentally, I was an immature and unhappy young lad. I wanted to receive love and compassion, and to have a good quality of life, but I was too stupid to realise that abusing my family members is not the way to gain it.

During this time, a spirit of fear consumed me, which manifested itself most clearly when we were on holidays in Portrush. I simply refused to leave the caravan while the others enjoyed shopping, the beach, or other amusements. I never told anyone, but I feared meeting anyone I knew from school. I went out on the first day and saw a kid from the year below me. I didn't want to run into him or anyone else again. It was stupid because he was a nice guy who chatted to me in school and didn't do anything wrong. I ruined a lovely holiday for myself for no good reason. I was in turmoil.

Worse was yet to come. When I was fifteen, just about to turn sixteen, a letter came through our door. It was written by a highly respected paediatrician to my doctor. It contained an assessment of my abilities: 'Joseph's intelligence is below normal. He is slow to learn.'

I was furious and demanded, 'Who wrote this?'

Mum tried to defuse the situation patiently explain. 'One doctor was writing to another. You shouldn't worry about it.'

I was incensed. Didn't they know I was top of the class at school? Less than eight years earlier, I was written about in the papers as a 'very bright boy'.

Dad, I think, felt that the letter was my just desserts and hoped that it would bring me back to earth with a jolt. He was right. It did and has since been replaced by two university certificates. At the time, however, it fuelled my anger.

My behaviour at home became so bad that my parents asked a paediatrician for help. She referred me to a Centre of Troubled Children and Adolescents in Antrim. I hated going there and once again felt like I was being punished while the true perpetrators were being ignored. The counsellor I met there, a middle-aged man with a strong Republic of Ireland accent, seemed at first to be ignorant and aloof to what I was saying.

During one of our early sessions, he asked me what a week looked like for me. When I recounted what I did over the prior seven days, he responded, 'You sound like a computer, not a human being.'

Outwardly, I may have apologised but inwardly I was

thinking, *You are an ignorant Southern fool, I really don't care what you think.*

In other sessions, he referred to some of my answers as rubbish. Of course, I resented his assessment. *One man's rubbish is another man's treasure.*

Over time, though, I grew to respect at least some of what the counsellor said. For example, he insisted on confidentiality between us. I appreciated that. And in what was our final meeting, he said something I tried to deny but was fully true. 'Joseph, are you angry about having a disability that stops you from doing some of the things you want to do? If you are, that's okay, because if I had a disability like yours, I would be as mad, too.'

That admission has stayed with me to this day. It assured me that sometimes it is okay to be angry, to admit when life gets too much and that I need help. What I needed to change was the way I reacted in situations when I felt sad or hurt.

Soon afterwards, Mum and Dad decided that as my behaviour had been reasonable for a while, I would not have to go back to the Centre for Troubled Adolescents in Antrim.

Just a short time later, a visit to the orthopaedic surgeon's clinic would test my resolve to be more constructive and, in the short-term at least, do something to calm my troubled soul.

CHAPTER ELEVEN

'HE NEEDS ANOTHER OPERATION'

My Most Painful Place

The orthopaedic surgeon who performed all three of my surgeries held a regular clinic at Fleming Fulton. The Boss, as he always signed my plaster casts, was an excellent practitioner and I loved seeing him. For several years following my foot alignment surgery, he was happy to simply let the physiotherapists work with me.

By the time I had reached year four in secondary school, however, he had determined that my muscles had tightened to the point where it became necessary to repeat the hamstring lengthening operation he had done on me around ten years earlier.

I had been dreading this news, although it was not entirely unexpected. My knees and legs had become increasingly painful, my walking was poor, and I was stubbornly refusing to do my exercises.

Mum usually accompanied me up to Belfast for my appointments, but she couldn't on this occasion, so I attended the clinic on my own. I was absolutely terrified of having to go home and deliver to my parents the news of my needing another surgery. Mum had warned me for quite some time that if I didn't do my exercises, I would end up back in hospital. Dad always said that if I ended up back in Musgrave Park again, 'lying gurning' as he put it, he would not drive all the way up to Belfast to visit me. I ignored their warnings, thinking arrogantly that it wouldn't happen to me.

Aware of my concern, the school physiotherapist promised to ring Mum before I arrived home and tell her what the doctor said, but for some reason, she was unable to make contact, which left me to tell Mum myself. Her immediate reaction was resignation rather than anger. Most children with cerebral palsy require a repeat operation on their hamstrings during their mid-teens since this age experiences a period of physical growth. Perhaps my parents were unaware of this, or maybe they hoped to avoid it if I maintained my exercise regime.

The date for my third operation was set relatively quickly. A letter arrived on the last day of school before the Christmas holidays in 1992 I was scheduled for surgery in the second week of January.

That Christmas was happy and uneventful. I came

down with a bad cough and head cold just after the New Year. Mum hoped it would clear up in time for the surgery. She made me go out for a walk with her in the cold winter air, saying with a smile, 'This will either cure you or kill you, Joseph.' Privately I wouldn't have minded the latter outcome, as I wasn't looking forward to going into hospital.

Much to my disappointment, that walk did the trick, and I was taken to hospital the following Monday, 4 January 1993, for a two-week stay. As Mum left my bedside the first evening, any pretences I had about being a big, hard lad disappeared. I kissed her for the first time in several years and reached forward eagerly for a hug. Later that night, I cried like a baby to the nurses on duty. Alice and Bridie were lovely older women who held my hand and talked to me all night. Several other nurses, including Susan, Julie, and Mary, were equally kind to me throughout my stay.

The next morning, one of the nurses took me into the shower cubicles. It then struck me just how important the impending surgery was. I couldn't walk unaided from my bed on the ward to the shower, which was just down the corridor. The pain I experienced in that short distance drove home to me just how much I needed the operation.

The next day, Mum's birthday, she arrived in the company of a lovely wee Presbyterian Deaconess who prayed for us before leaving to let Mum and me talk about the surgery.

Eventually, the porters arrived to take to me to the operating theatre. I got one last kiss from Mum before being wheeled away. All too quickly I arrived at my destination where The Boss was waiting with his team.

'Hello, Joseph. Try not to be worried. This man here'—he looked to the anaesthetist—'is going to put you to sleep.'

With that, the anaesthetist placed a large mask over my face and I immediately tasted gas. Desperate to gag, I heard him say, 'It's okay. Count from ten to one.'

I did as instructed. 'Ten, nine, eig . . .'

The next thing I remember was waking up in the recovery room. I was groggy, tired, and sore. I wanted to back to sleep. All I felt below my waist was pain, thinly masked by heavy plaster casts. I don't remember if I saw Mum that night, but I am sure she was there.

A couple of days later I told Mum that I had never experienced pain like it in my life. She said, 'Oh, you probably did. You just don't remember it!'

My recovery from that operation seemed slow. I was in pain for several days afterwards and didn't want to do anything. One highlight of my hospital stay was the visit by the cast of *Aladdin*, who was in pantomime at the Lyric theatre. They signed a get-well card for me. That same day, some pupils from school with whom I had just performed *Aladdin* in the Christmas show came by to see me. They were older kids, not my tormentors. It was nice to see familiar faces.

My time in Musgrave was also important because it provided me with an opportunity to meet a man who would become hugely significant in my life over the next twenty-five years. Rev Brian Boyd had just been installed as the minister of Kells and Eskylane Presbyterian churches. I loved Brian from the moment I met him and would defy anyone not to! He had a lovely, warm-hearted presence about him. He was, and still is, a gentleman in every sense of the word.

It blew me away that a minister would make anything other than a token visit to a fourteen-year-old boy in hospital. Remarkably, he stayed with me for over an hour on each of his two visits to Musgrave, making a massive impression on me. I may not have eventually found my way back to God without his genuine care. Although gentle, Brian did not mince his words, even as I lay on that hospital bed. After a bit of chat about football, he turned the conversation to church. 'Are you saved, Joseph?'

'Yes, I am. But I haven't really been taking much notice of God for a while.'

Brian smiled as if he already knew my answer. 'God still loves you and hasn't forgotten you. Sometimes He allows things like this [operation] to happen as a reminder that He is still here. But this is not a punishment. Now you might be wishing that the surgeons had left you alone, but the operation will help you to feel stronger.'

For the rest of my hospital visit and perhaps a day

or two afterwards, I went through what I call a God phase. Nurse Bridie even remarked about it. 'You have a gift for sharing the gospel.' At that moment, I had good intentions of being obedient to the Lord, but it would be at least a couple more years before I would truly surrender to him.

CHAPTER TWELVE

'YOU DID REALLY WELL'

Entering a Place of Recovery

When I returned to school after my operation, the physiotherapists' care and rehabilitation were outstanding.

Six weeks after surgery the plaster was removed, but I found it impossible to bend my knee or straighten it without extreme pain. Even thinking about it now makes me wince. I have never, ever felt such anguish in my life. Think of a thousand hot pokers going right through your bones.

The agony I experienced set back my recovery. For days and weeks afterwards, I was too frightened to move for fear of the pain. However, the physiotherapists were patient with me, careful to praise even the smallest attempt at movement. The hydrotherapist said to me in front of her colleagues,

'You did really well in the pool yesterday.' I was grateful for her encouragement.

One distinct advantage of being at a school for physically disabled children and young people is that, in most cases, physical, occupational, and other therapeutic services are available on site and free of charge. I and countless others were blessed by this provision. Having it available meant that I was released from hospital more quickly and received daily sessions with caring professionals whom I knew and trusted.

Post-operative physio began with hydrotherapy. The heated water eased the pain in my joints, making movement easier. The initial water-based exercises focussed on non-weight-bearing activities, where I was encouraged to kick. Then I was asked to try to walk in the shallow end, initially without resistance then gradually with resistance. Out of the water, the physio treated me to a slip board exercise to encourage more knee bending. Ouch! I had to lie on my stomach and bend back towards my hips. Resistance was added once my fuller range of movement returned. All of this was followed by exercises to improve my standing balance and relearning to walk, using a correct gait with step-led movements in which the distance quickly increased.

Within six weeks, I was walking with the aid of a four-wheeled walker. Eventually, I managed to walk unaided again. The lads with whom I participated in the lunchtime kick-about noticed that I had, however, lost a yard of pace!

Recovering from the surgery impacted my schoolwork. Struggling with GCSE Mathematics, I transferred to the City & Guilds Numeracy qualification, which suited me better. I took GCSE French and was awarded the school cup for my performance in class. My best subjects were English and History. Both teachers were excellent, and their confidence brought out the best in me.

One humorous piece I submitted for my GCSE English coursework was entitled 'I Have Never Been So Relieved'. My teacher claimed it as one of the best pieces of writing she had read for many years—funny, mature, and clever. Originally, the class had been asked to recount a stressful situation from which they had emerged unscathed. I wrote about my frustrations at not been able to recall a scenario and remarked at the end of the essay, 'I had never been so relieved to get a piece of writing done!'

My history course focussed on the two World Wars and finished by looking at the end of the Cold War. As someone with a keen interest in politics, I enjoyed this study. I also looked forward to Science, although I struggled with the practical side because my hands shake.

I emerged from Fifth Form with Cs in English and History, a D in Science, and an F for French. These marks were okay, given that they were Mode 2 exams, meaning that the highest grade I could attain was a C in each subject. Along with my City & Guilds

Numeracy, in which I was awarded a Distinction plus the Royal Society of Arts Computer Literacy and Information Technology certificate, my results were more than acceptable by Fleming Fulton standards. I would be allowed to take more GSCEs the following year, including Religious Education and English Literature, two subjects which I found extremely interesting. I had spoken to the English teacher, who was also my form tutor, about my ultimate desire to go to university. She confirmed that if I worked hard, I could attain this goal. She was a nice Christian woman who knew of my church connections and faith, albeit flimsy, in God, and she thought I should consider attending Bible college.

Encouraged by her words, I was already thinking of life beyond school. A lot had happened there, which I didn't want to be reminded of. A move to somewhere closer to home and away from this place where I had struggled for so long beckoned. I could imagine how God would use me there, even if He wasn't always at the forefront of my mind.

CHAPTER THIRTEEN

'IT'S NOT A SCHOOL; IT'S A TRAINING CENTRE'

Time to Switch Places?

The Northern Ireland Council for Orthopaedic Development (NICOD), which was rebranded as the Cedar Foundation in the late 1990s, runs a training centre in Ballymena. The centre, which opened in 1990 after years of lobbying by Ethel Kenny, offered vocational training opportunities in Catering, Business Administration, and Information for people with physical disabilities. It boasted an outstanding record in providing qualifications and pathways to employment. Mum heard about it through my aunt Mary. Soon a prospectus landed at our front door.

In keeping with my mood around April 1993 as I was approaching the end of Fourth Form, when Mum showed me the information, my answer was a flat

'No, I am not interested in that.' I shoved the book into the bottom of a cupboard. My anger was tied in with my attitude towards my disability. To be blunt, I hated that I was disabled. I wanted nothing to do with a place that was for disabled people, and, as I saw it, NICOD would mark me out as even more handicapped.

'You sent me to a rubbish disabled school where I am made to wear stupid callipers on my legs, and now you show me some dopey book about some dippy centre for handicapped people. Who do you think I am?' This was my typical response to those who tried to enthuse me about NICOD.

Admittedly, my mind-set was a stupid one. Loads of local summer schemes and other activities organised by Social Services in Ballymena were available that I could have gone to and enjoyed with many of the kids I knew from Beechgrove. However, I stubbornly refused to go, preferring to sit at home alone because I thought it made me seem more normal.

My attitude towards NICOD Centre began to improve for no other reason than I was bored during the school holidays. I fished the prospectus out of the cupboard and began to leaf through it. My eye was drawn towards a photo of someone I recognised: Ethel Kenny. She was pictured at the centre, and the caption below described her as a Member of NICOD's Executive Committee.

Her involvement piqued my interest. I became aware of an increasing number of articles in local newspapers hailing the centre's success. Those who attended were learning to drive, getting jobs, and doing everyday things. I was intrigued. And I wouldn't need to leave the house at 7.15 a.m. as I had done while attending Fleming Fulton in Belfast.

I gradually warmed to the idea of a move from Fleming Fulton to NICOD. I reasoned out that I would probably end up going there after I had finished my compulsory education. When my GSCE results from Fleming arrived a day behind Mark's, I convinced myself that staff there were being disrespectful to me and I would show them by leaving!

I rang up and made an appointment to visit NICOD Centre. The manager, Bernie Graffin, showed me around. As usual, I was shy and nervous during the visit, so Mum did most of the talking. I reckon that, while we did like the centre, neither of us knew whether I would end up there or not, particularly as the centre was oversubscribed and Bernie could not offer me five days a week of training.

School in Belfast resumed a few days later. My family and I decided not to tell them I had applied to go to NICOD Centre. After all, what if I didn't get accepted? How would I be treated at Fleming Fulton if they knew I was planning my escape?

About three weeks into the new term, I received a letter from NICOD inviting me to train two days per week in Business Administration. The information intimated that I could increase to a further two days in the centre's IT suite when a place became available.

Decision time. Did I stay at school or leave for NICOD? The letter had arrived on Friday. That evening I decided, 'Yes! Yes, I am definitely going.' By the time Sunday came, however, I was less sure. Indeed, I cried to my parents that I wanted to stay at school because I was afraid that 'I couldn't cope at NICOD.' Mum and Dad's initial reaction was frustration, understandably so, given my behaviour over recent years and how I expressed daily my hatred of Fleming Fulton.

'You have gurned and moaned about that school every day since you have been there, and now when you have the chance to leave you won't. You know there is a waiting list to get into NICOD. If you don't go when you are asked, you won't get in later. They can fill their places with the click of a finger.' He snapped his fingers.

Once my parents calmed down, they apologised for their reactions and assured me that they would not pressure me either way. I was torn between the devil I knew and the devil I did not. Also, I didn't see myself in an office situation, which was the heart of the Business Administration training I was being offered. I wanted university and journalism. When the decisive moment came, I opted to go to NICOD. Part of my decision was based on wanting to appear like a grown-up seventeen-year-old, even though I was an immature, sheltered boy who was scared of failure. I hoped that a fresh start somewhere, anywhere, would erase all the bad memories and problems I had accumulated since leaving Beechgrove years earlier.

Into school I went the following Monday with a discharge letter from my parents in hand.

'Why are you leaving?' my bemused form tutor asked. 'The package of qualifications you asked for last year has been put in place for you here. Why didn't you say in June that you wanted to go? There would have been no problem.'

Another senior teacher remarked, 'Joseph, I think you are only thinking short-term. You want out of here, but where will you be in a couple of years?'

Finally, the head of the school's Secondary Department said, 'Please understand that we are not just trying to keep you, but we want to you to be sure that you are making the right decision for your future.'

My responses to these remarks ranged from 'It's too long a journey to travel to school each morning. I am tired of the travelling' to 'I have never really fit in here. I want to be with people who share my country accent and live close by. I am going to keep learning; it just won't be here.' Blah . . . blah . . . blah . . .

There was more than a grain of truth in my answers. I didn't feel that I could fit in with people in a city thirty miles from my hometown. I had been physically, emotionally, and verbally bullied by some of my fellow pupils at the school because I was polite to the teachers, answered questions in class, and wanted to learn. During the summer, I had received some external examination results a day later than my able-bodied twin brother, Mark, because my school sent them out by second-class post rather than using the first class delivery system adopted by every other school in Northern Ireland, which ensured that students received their examination results on the day they were first made available 'That's the respect they have for you,' exclaimed Mark when he saw the delayed postmark of the envelope. His advice to Mum was, 'Ring Fleming Fulton. Tell them he is leaving and tell them why.'

In hindsight, my decision to leave school was the right one, and I believe God engineered it for the good of myself and others. That said, I do regret the way in which I left school. To walk into the place where I had spent most days over a six-year period and simply say 'I'm leaving' was bad form on my part and certainly did not show any evidence of God in my life. Though much of my time there had been difficult, and the staff weren't perfect and may not have understood me, none intended me any harm. I should have been more upfront and honest about my intentions and unhappiness. Had I done so, I could have left with more courtesy.

In the late 1980s when I chose to attend Fleming Fulton as an eleven-year-old, relatively few mainstream schools could accept pupils with a disability. Mitchell House in Belfast was an alternative; however, it did not offer much for brighter pupils, and it would have probably left me even more frustrated, albeit in a different way. I enjoyed succeeding at school, and

Fleming Fulton had afforded me a taste of that. In a situation where few options existed, I had made the best decision I could. Leaving my school for NICOD also turned out to be the right call. With the pace of learning at my school, I would never have attained the qualifications needed to go from there straight to university. The local further education college was not, at that time, ready to fill the gap. My only regret was the way my departure played out.

***

I arrived at NICOD Training Centre on the first Tuesday of October 1994. A black car bearing the sign of a local taxi firm pulled up into the housing estate where I lived. Not realising exactly where my house was, the driver stopped at the bottom of the development. Knowing that the vehicle was for me, I walked over and got in. The driver was a friendly guy who introduced himself and the others in the car, who were also NICOD bound.

I asked one of my fellow passengers, 'Is NICOD all right?'

'It's like everything else. You get cheesed off with it.'

His terse reply shook me. I nodded as if to say I understood, but inside I felt dread. What had I got myself into?

Around twenty minutes later, we arrived at the centre where the Business Administration tutor stood ready to welcome me warmly. He showed me around the building before settling me at a desk and giving me a National Vocational Qualification (NVQ) Level One Business Administration workbook. My new chapter in education had begun.

Morning tea and lunch were cooked on the premises. The food served in the canteen was far superior to the bland school dinners I had become accustomed to. Equally refreshing was that there were no bullies. The people were pleasant. Indeed, they were more than civil and tolerant of a socially naïve seventeen-year-old who didn't know much about anything outside of school, church, or Boys Brigade.

The same guy who told me that you could get 'cheesed off at' NICOD was full of praise for the centre by the end of my first week there. 'You like it?' he asked me. 'Aye, they are all dead on—very patient, and it beats sitting in the house!'

'Yeah. They all seem nice. The girl who teaches Business Admin seems all right, and the food in the canteen is nicer than the last school I was at.'

The man, who was in his thirties, with a young family, smiled. 'I'm glad you like it, but you have got your terminology wrong. It's not a school; it's a training centre. You can think for yourself. We are all grown-ups.'

I was certainly beginning to feel more grown up. Decreased tension in my day-to-day life meant that I felt less angry, and I became easier to live with at home. Though I could still be a moody teenager, I didn't hate the world as I had before.

My only issue with NICOD concerned the range of

careers and subjects for which training was available. Neither was I particularly proficient in many of the tasks required of me. I struggled to get the hang of transferring telephone calls from reception to other parts of the building. I photocopied everything upside down and stapled booklets in the wrong order. I wasn't messing about and I genuinely wanted to do better, but I just kept getting muddled. To use a Ballymena phrase: I was handless!

I was still dreaming of university and becoming a journalist, a fact which probably didn't help me to concentrate on operating the photocopier! Opportunities to fulfil my aspirations seemed less available by the day.

One Thursday afternoon as I was carrying out a stock inventory in the stationery store for my NVQ file, I had an unexpected experience. Having grown up in a Presbyterian church, I wasn't accustomed to getting a word from God or hearing His voice audibly, but for a few seconds, I heard something from within me say: *Is this it, Joe? All the ability you have been given and you are trying to carve out a niche for yourself as the storeman at NICOD? Really?*

Something had to change. Quickly.

CHAPTER FOURTEEN

'I DON'T THINK WE CAN HELP YOU HERE'

A Place of Dejection

After about three minutes of thought, I decided to enrol at the Ballymena campus of the North-East Institute of Further and Higher Education to study for GCSEs and A-Levels while still attending the NICOD Training Centre.

I rang the college and set up an appointment to meet with Mrs. Atkinson the following Friday. *This should be straightforward, I thought. I will attend the North-East Institute in Ballymena, they will immediately accept me, I will do a few GCSEs this year, A-Levels in the next year: university and reporting, here I come!*

Unfortunately, reality was not what I expected. Flanked by my mum, I entered the ancient-looking, austere, grey college building. The receptionist told us to wait, that she would let Mrs. Atkinson know we had arrived.

Following what seemed like an unusually long wait, a woman who appeared to be in her forties approached us. Her shoulder length hair was dyed ash-blonde, and she was dressed in a grey trouser-suit. 'I think you might be here to see me,' she said, her voice quiet and polite but somewhat hurried and apologetic. Her tense face had the look of someone who had somewhere else to be but was squeezing me into her schedule to avoid being rude.

'Let's sit over here for a few minutes.' She beckoned us into a small booth in the Student Services office. 'Now, tell me why you are here today. I understand you have just left school, is that right?'

'Yes, I was at Fleming Fulton in Belfast,' I stammered. 'But I didn't like it. It was too far from home; they didn't teach us much. I am at NICOD Centre at the minute, but I want to study for my GCSEs and be a journalist.'

Mrs. Atkinson listened attentively, but her demeanour was far from positive. As soon as I had finished speaking, she looked at Mum and me and said, 'I am afraid that all our GCSE classes have started and are full. You would already be behind. Another problem is that the lift here is broken at the minute and the stairs are steep. We also have long corridors. I would be worried about you falling and having an accident.'

Then came a comment that kicked me right in the

guts. 'Fleming Fulton offer some GCSEs. Your best bet is to go back there. Would they take you back?'

I looked at Mum and she at me. In unison and with weak voices, we said, 'No.'

I answered based on pride rather than knowledge of whether or not I could re-enter the special school I had discarded just two weeks earlier. No way would I have had the courage to ask for a return.

'That's a pity because I don't think we can help you here. I am sorry.'

Arm in arm, Mum and I walked out the building and back to the car. I felt utterly broken inside. My heart felt like a brick inside my chest. Sick and weak, my stomach felt completely empty. Tears gathered behind my eyes, invisible for that moment but not for long.

'Well, that's that, Joseph. You may get down on your knees and beg for those extra days she promised you.' Mum was referring to Bernie Graffin, who had promised that my two-days-per-week placement at NICOD would increase to four as soon as possible.

I didn't say much in reply. Inside my head, I was scrambling to salvage something from the day. At some point during the homeward car journey we talked about the possibility of my going to the North-East Institute's campus in the neighbouring town of Antrim. We knew someone with a disability who had studied there. I resolved to make an appointment with the Admissions Team there when I got home. Whatever I was feeling in my heart, I knew that I couldn't surrender my dream.

As soon as I got through the front door, I rang the college in Antrim and made a date to visit it. From my position in the hallway, I heard Mum and Mark discussing how the day had gone. I resented his involvement at that point. *It was all right for him. Grammar school kid, he's doing his A-Levels. He's going to university—Mum and Dad's pride and joy looking down on me. It's not my fault I am disabled and had to go a rubbish special school.*

I put down the telephone and said to Mum, 'I have got an appointment at Antrim Tech next week.'

'So, it's another operation like today then?' Her lack of enthusiasm was clear.

I sat at the lunch table a few minutes later, talking up the appointment with my voice while my eyes showed obvious disappointment. Mum's concluding comment, said in love, 'Again, Joseph, you may get down on your knees and beg for those extra days at NICOD.'

I turned my back and trudged down to the bedroom I shared with Mark. I wanted to be on my own. Thankfully, he had gone out. I looked at the red National Record of Achievement I had received from Fleming Fulton just a few weeks earlier. The comments from my teachers were positive, and my ears rang with the voices of the concerned and kind professionals at the special school I had walked away from, urging me to rethink my decision. I thought of the classmates I had left behind in Belfast. It was

Friday. They would be playing football right now, having a laugh. They had choices and they had one another. I was in my shared bedroom flicking through a book showing my underwhelming list of qualifications. I had landed myself at a place where people were kind enough, more than civil, but barring the Ballymena accents, I had little in common with them. The Business Administration course I was doing there was not suiting me, and even if it worked out, what was the best I could achieve long-term? Filing and photocopying in office. Big deal!

I thought back to playing football at school, remembered the teachers who praised my work. I cast my mind further to primary school, where I was thought to be a bit of a superstar. I was asked to write an article for a local newspaper as an eight-year-old. I was a clever boy who was going to do great things. *What had gone wrong in just a few years, even just a fortnight? It's all over; no university, no reporting, just NICOD, and I am not good there.* I crumpled on my bed and cried bitterly and intensely. I lifted my eyes briefly to see my red bloodshot face in the mirror. My jacket was wet with tears.

My problems were by no means of that moment alone. I had been struggling for a few years beforehand. Being top of the class academically in a special school was no big achievement. Some of my peers there couldn't read; others were too immature and spoilt to care. I had been bullied, and my behaviour at home was so worrying that I had been sent to a unit for troubled children and adolescents as an out-patient. However, now in October 1994, when I caught myself in the mirror, everything just seemed to hit me.

Then the same voice who spoke to me while at NICOD doing inventory said, *Surrender to God and you will find a way out of this; don't and you will end up with nothing. Absolutely nothing.*

Remembering the commitment I made to Jesus as a six-year-old, I said, 'God, I am sorry. I promise I will do whatever You say from now on. Just get me out of this hole. Give me back my ability, my writing, my future, and I will be Yours. I promise. I used to be Your best and brightest boy. Take me back there, I beg You.'

CHAPTER FIFTEEN

'YOU AIM VERY HIGH, JOE'

An Open Door to New Heights

Even after I prayed to God, begging Him to restore my academic fortunes, I would be lying if I said that my heart and attitude were transformed in a single second. I was still an immature seventeen-year-old who was wet behind the ears from having led a sheltered existence. That said, God rekindled a spark in me. I wanted to do something with my life. I just wasn't entirely sure how I was going to get there or even what 'there' looked like.

I spoke to someone from the North-East Institute's Antrim Campus who told me that I could undertake GCSEs through a distance-learning programme, which involved attending the campus once a month and completing my coursework at home

That seemed doable, although I was advised not to

start the programme until the following September because the course had already begun for that year. For months, I held on to the booklet outlining the available subjects. I didn't care what I studied, I just wanted GCSEs to enable me to move on to A-Levels and then go to this magical place called university (as I perceived it), where I would be recognised as smart, not stupid, and respected rather than ridiculed.

Looking back over the past twenty-five years, my long relationship with God has shown me that nothing happens by chance. He has a plan for those who follow Him. I may be the stereotypical Israelite from Exodus whose disobedient arrogance forced God to take him through a long wilderness before allowing him to enter the promised land, but lead me He did. His method, however, seemed at the time to come out of the blue.

I was channel flicking on my bedroom TV one Monday afternoon when I came across an advertisement for the Open University. I knew about it because of the boring programmes that aired every Saturday morning before the cartoons I watched as a child. Of course, I understood not a word of them as a six-year-old, but the clip I watched in my late teens caught my attention. The people on the ad said, 'I used to have a boring existence with a rubbish job, but then I found out about the Open University. And now I have a degree and the life I have always wanted. You can do the same! Sign up today!'

Almost immediately, I jotted down the telephone

number that flashed on the screen and ordered my introductory prospectus. Days later, a shiny catalogue-style book arrived. It was full of people talking about how the Open University had changed their lives and enabled them to get the job of their dreams. I flicked to the outlines of the offered courses. Mathematics and French seemed too complex, and traditional science seemed dull. I kept reading until I got to a page describing the Social Science Foundation course. The text spoke about how students would be studying people, politics, the history behind government policy, etc. All these areas interested me and seemed simpler than the other courses—at least I understood the synopsis!

I ordered a more specific course catalogue. Once I read it, I made up my mind. I was going to enrol to study at the Social Science at the Open University, I was going to succeed, and I knew my next step.

Reaction to my sudden change of direction was mixed, to put it mildly. Dad said, 'Son, you see that stuff you got from the Open University? Throw it in the fire; it's rubbish.'

Staff at the training centre seemed equally worried when I raced in the following day with news of my master plan. 'You are aiming very high, Joe,' one said. 'Do you not think it is a massive jump from O-Levels to doing a degree?' another asked. Bernie Graffin, the centre's manager, drew me a diagram featuring two circular islands, one representing where I was presently and the other depicting where I wanted to be: a graduate journalist. Between the circles, Bernie drew a bridge, which she said represented taking the conventional route to third-level education, which was strewn with GCSEs followed by A-Levels. Trying to reach my preferred destination through the Open University (OU) was, she argued, akin to jumping into the sea and attempting to swim to the island of success—a risky manoeuvre. However, if I was patient enough to use the bridge, I was 'almost certain to succeed.'

My response to all these negative comments was something like 'I believe I can make it. Other people do. This will get me a degree. Let me prove it to you.'

While I was telling everyone that I could complete my OU course, I wasn't sure in my own mind that I could. I was trying to convince myself that it was the right thing to do. That little voice inside told me that I was capable of more than my current situation suggested, but what this meant I was not sure.

NICOD staff were correct to warn me about the potential pitfalls of attempting a degree level course with only a handful of average GCSEs to my name. They didn't know me as the talented young boy from Beechgrove who wrote stories good enough to be published. I stood before them as a shy, sometimes stammering, seventeen-year-old who had crashed out of school just a month or two before. They went as far as sharing with me their concerns that if I started a degree course I was later unable to finish, the impact of such a failure on my self-esteem would be catastrophic for me. In truth, they were probably right. If I abandoned my NVQ to sign up for a course I couldn't finish, I would end up with nothing.

***

Closing my eyes and ears to all the naysayers, something from within me, which I now truly believe to be the promptings of the Spirit of God, kept my mind set on the path to the OU. I went to their Ballymena Information Evening and signed up for the first term, which began in February 1996.

The tutorials were held in a local high school about ten minutes by car from my home. In Foundation Course year, these two-hour sessions took place on an almost weekly basis, which was invaluable to me. The tutor, a middle-aged man in his late forties or early fifties, was friendly and patient in class, although somewhat notorious in OU circles for marking essays rather severely! My fellow students appeared to be in their thirties and forties. I enjoyed these early classes. I thrived in my independence. I loved learning and debating. My first Tutor-Marked Assignment (TMA) received 59 percent. I followed this with marks of 50, 47, 45, 39, 70, 55, and 51. All but one was a pass grade, and I should have done better in the failed assignment in which I had scored only 39 percent. I had gone off on a tangent during the essay, thinking my answer needed to be more complex than it should have been. I learned my lesson and finished the year with a coursework average of 52 percent, 12 percent above the pass mark. Because of my disability and the need of a computer to write, the instructor gave me the option of doing my examination at home under the supervision of an invigilator appointed by the university. For the first four years, Margaret, who worked in the Study Support section of the OU in Belfast, came to my home during examinations. I took my end-of-year exam in October 1996, and after several anxious weeks of waiting, the results arrived by post just before Christmas. I passed with a very convincing 47 percent. I was thrilled to get through the Foundation Course and quickly set about choosing my second-year modules.

Back at NICOD, my academic progress was not going unnoticed. Centre staff could not have been more helpful or encouraging with my studies. They saw that I was struggling with the practical demands of office work and recognised that my Business Administration career path was not fulfilling me. They happily proofread my essays, offering guidance where they could, and helped me to fill in any handwritten forms. Not all the employees there were Christians, but it is fair to say that God used them to restore my academic and career prospects. I would not have been able to achieve what I did without the help of those dedicated professionals.

The encouragement they gave me coupled with the pass grade I had achieved from my first-year OU studies were key in boosting my self-esteem and cooling my internal anger further. The work and effort I put into my degree course were beginning to earn me respect within my family. Slowly, my relationships with Mum, Dad, and my siblings continued to improve.

My interest in writing had not waned. During one of her occasional visits to the training centre, Ethel Kenny asked me, 'How are you getting on with your work, Joe? Are you training to be the great journalist I told you that you would be from you were five years old?'

For a brief time, I endeavoured to put journalism to the back of my mind. Well-meaning people had tried to tell me how difficult it would be to make my mark in this profession given my circumstances. I couldn't physically write, so shorthand was impossible. A year of driving lessons had shown that my damaged brain couldn't cope with the demands of driving. So how could I get around to cover stories? I also walk with a stagger, so depending on my legs to get me from one place to another was not an option. Try as I might, however, I couldn't stop thinking about writing as a career. Dreams re-awakened. Somehow, I knew I would make my career as a reporter happen. I had always felt that journalism was my destiny, and nothing else captured my imagination.

The staff at NICOD worked hard to support my ambitions. The Job Coach, Robert Wilson, a lovely Christian guy whom God placed in my path, along with Bernie Graffin decided to establish a newsletter, which the trainees and staff of the Ballymena centre would write. They appointed me editor. I stepped into my element. We featured 'exclusive' interviews with the staff about their roles; trainees talked about their programmes; and, of course, I had my own column, 'Boyd's Bit', in which I mused about disability affairs like benefits, education, or whatever else was in my head!

We named the newsletter *Focus on NICOD.* It gave me the opportunity to seek out and write about things that had affected me. Despite my success with the OU, I had not forgotten my demeaning experience during my visit to the local further education college. I was determined that being discouraged to enrol based on disability would not happen to anyone else, and our newsletter gave me the chance to play my part in changing attitudes and, hopefully, lives forever.

CHAPTER SIXTEEN

'WE SHOULD BE ENCOURAGING ALL STUDENTS, WHATEVER THEIR NEED'

Changing Places

Following my unsuccessful attempt to enrol at the North-East Institute of Further and Higher Education, I recognised an issue that needed to be addressed. I became vocal, stressing to anyone who would listen how unfair it was that a college could get away with discouraging people from enrolling, claiming the facilities were inaccessible to those with physical disabilities.

Whether because of a desire to shut me up or to enact positive change, a staff member at NICOD made what would be a policy-changing suggestion for both the charity and our town's college.

'You and Robert [Job Coach at the centre] should

go and meet with the director of the college. Seriously, write her a letter asking for an appointment and be sure to mark it confidential if you don't want anyone else to see it.'

For a teenager to go to the head of a major regional college seemed intimidating, but the prospect excited me. After consulting Robert, I wrote to the director explaining that I was editor of the *Focus on NICOD* newsletter and asking if I could interview her regarding what the college offered to trainees within our organisation.

A few weeks later, I was at the centre when a phone call was put through the Business Administration Section for me. It was the director of the North-East Institute ringing to offer me an appointment. Wow! I pushed down my star-struck excitement long enough to take the date for the appointment and finish the conversation.

Nervous and full of anticipation, I ran to the office. 'Robert! Robert, I have just had a phone call from the head of the local college. She would like to see me in a couple of weeks. Can you come with me?'

After checking his diary, Robert agreed. The countdown to the biggest interview of my fledgling career began. In the fortnight that followed, I worked hard with Robert to prepare. He emphasised the need for me to be respectful and fair with the college principal. It would not, he suggested, further my cause if I went into the interview with a determination to tear her apart in revenge for what happened to me.

I understood what Robert was saying and I agreed.

I also saw the importance of allowing others to contribute to the process, so I went around collecting questions for the interview from my fellow trainees as well as NICOD staff members.

Finally, the big day arrived. I even wore a suit! I had a physiotherapy appointment in the morning, so I arrived at NICOD around lunchtime to meet Robert and travel to our meeting at the college. The director's PA met us and showed us into her boss's office. A few moments later, a middle-aged lady with a strong Welsh accent entered the room and introduced herself and another woman, a senior member of the teaching staff.

'Now, tell me about yourselves,' the lady said, her voice gentle and her demeanour friendly.

I explained that I was a trainee at the NICOD Centre in Ballymena for people with physical disabilities. Robert introduced himself as the Job Support Worker, whose role was to support trainees as they got to grips with job roles in the workplace.

Making notes, the college Director smiled. 'Why have you come to see me today?'

I explained about my article for the training centre's magazine to inform my fellow trainees what the North-East Institute offered them. I further explained that I and a few others from NICOD had endured less than positive experiences at the college and asked what her message was to disabled people who wish to study there.

She sat back in her chair. 'I think that we should be encouraging everyone to attend the North-East Institute whether they have a disability or not, because everyone has a special need of some kind. We want to see to it that disabled people are represented within the main student body.'

I asked what the college was doing to bring about the day of equality between students with disabilities and their able-bodied counterparts.

The director and her colleague explained how they were working to improve the provision for disabled people within the college. They spoke about the availability of loop systems for the deaf, notetakers for people who couldn't write, assessible toilets, and disabled parking spaces at the college door. The principal was also keen to stress that she had been instructing caretakers to ensure that no able-bodied drivers used these unfairly. Her colleague chipped. 'The group we let down the most are single parents, who experience issues securing child care while they study.'

I went on to ask practical questions as requested by my fellow trainees, such as whether there was a lift at the campus closest to them. One question, given to me by a young man who had enrolled to study for a B-Tec qualification, had to do with his experience of having to drop out because the tutor had been unable to source a laptop for him. The director expressed her regret and quipped, 'I would have brought my own laptop if I'd had known.'

Her colleague added, 'Joe, perhaps the message

here is to let us know as early as possible if a student has a particular need.'

In closing, I asked the director what her message was to any person with a disability who wished to enrol one of the North-East Institute's campuses. 'Come to the North-East Institute because we would be very supportive of students who have a special need.'

Robert and I left the interview feeling that we had been given a fair hearing and that college management genuinely wanted people with disabilities to enrol. Interestingly, when I sent the article to the director to sign off on it, my closing sentence read 'Come and see what we have on offer at the North-East Institute, because we would wish to be very supportive of students who have a special need.'

That alteration aside, a couple of very important things emerged from the interview. One of significance for me became evident in a post-interview remark from the director's colleague filtered back to me through a NICOD staff member. She was reported to have said, 'The young fellow, Joe, got as many answers from the director as I have ever heard her give anyone. He put her at ease but did it in such a way that he got her to answer the questions he asked her directly—he is a little bit cunning.'

I believe she meant those words as a compliment. The way I conducted our interview showed that I wasn't a pushover for authority figures. Nor was I just a fiery young disability campaigner with nothing to bring to the table. I had the ability to speak to people on any level, speak to them with courtesy, while also getting them to open up to me. This is an important attribute for any aspiring journalist and demonstrated potential success in my desired field.

A second important outcome from my interview had wide ramifications for the local disabled community. Following my meeting with the college director and her assurances that mainstream further education was available to students with disabilities, she and the NICOD director met together several times. As a result, they instituted a plan whereby trainees from the centre could undertake their chosen qualifications at the college with support from NICOD's Ballymena-based staff. I, along with a few others, were the first trainees to be sent to the college. At first the large building with long corridors were intimidating, but my nerves eased with time.

Since then I, along with many others, have attended the college sporadically over the years to study for qualifications in Counselling, Information Technology, and Languages. I recognise that the process is not always seamless, and much remains to be done by colleges, disability organisations, and individuals with disabilities. However, because of the courage God gave me in the interview, no person with a special need can be turned away at the door of their local education provider again. I am proud to have played my part in this.

God was helping me to make my mark and would soon open the door to more exciting opportunities.

CHAPTER SEVENTEEN

TIME FOR A CHANGE

My New Place

My interview with the director of the North-East Institute raised eyebrows in a positive way, and I was soon given the job of writing press releases for the local weekly newspapers in Ballymena on behalf of the training centre.

Although both publications were extremely supportive towards NICOD, I quickly developed a personal preference for the *Ballymena Times*. They published verbatim most of the pieces I wrote, and the paper always gave our articles prominent placing.

One Friday morning on arriving at NICOD, a delighted Robert greeted me and showed me a copy of the *Times* with my article and photo displayed proudly on the front page. I was thrilled and quick to show it off to everyone I knew.

Late 1996, Robert and I were tentatively discussing what I would do after I left NICOD the following October. Robert was charged with finding me a work placement that would develop my skills. Knowing my passion for writing, he contacted the *Ballymena Times* and arranged a meeting for us with the then editor Dessie Blackadder. The interview was set for the third Friday of January 1997.

Travelling to the newspaper office that day, Robert gave me a piece of advice. 'Joe, I can't make you any promises about this, but I fancy that if you impress him and get your foot in the door, there may be an opportunity for a regular column.'

Very soon, we arrived at the reception desk and asked to see the editor. The receptionist lifted her telephone. 'Dessie, there are two gentlemen from NICOD here to see you.'

A few minutes later, a young, slightly built man with brown hair rushed down the stairs. 'Hi, I am Dessie Blackadder. My office is just up the stairs. Will you be able to manage?' He looked to me.

'No problem,' I replied. I climbed the stairs, using the bannister for support, as Dessie apologised for the inaccessible nature of the building.

With the ascent complete, we entered Dessie's office. It mirrored the rest of the building. A dimly lit space that looked as if it was from a bygone era.

Robert, Dessie, and I sat down at a coffee table and began to talk about what had brought us to the point of this conversation.

While clearing space on the table, which was cluttered with newspaper, press releases, and Letters to the Editor, he looked at one of them and smiled. 'We spent our lives trying to decipher people's handwriting. Thankfully, we never have that problem with stuff from NICOD, which always comes in well-typed and readable.'

Robert grinned, pointing towards me. 'Joe writes most of those.'

'Do you enjoy writing, Joe?' Dessie enquired.

'Yes. It is something I have always enjoyed since I was a kid. I like to write for the magazine at the training centre.' I showed him a small portfolio of work I had collated in preparation—a few published press releases in addition to several copies of *Focus on NICOD*.

Keen that the editor should see my best work, Robert leafed through the pages and pulled out the my interview with the director of the North-East Institute. He handed it to Dessie, who nodded as he read it.

Then Dessie's eye turned to one of my 'Boyd's Bit' articles, where I had urged disabled people to stop sitting around waiting for things to happen, to get out, and try to live their own lives.

Dessie looked up at me. 'Do you know what we are missing?' He didn't wait for me to respond before going on. 'Is a bit of a ranter and a raver.' Turning to another gentler piece, he remarked, 'With all the council news we have to report, it would be nice to have someone to write something lighter, like what happened in Coronation Street last night.

'Yes, we could work on getting your typing speed up. I will take your file and show it to my editorial director so that he knows I am bringing in someone capable, not just a token disabled person, if you know what I mean?'

Robert and I nodded as Dessie beckoned us into the main editorial rooms to meet the crew. My eyes were like saucers as the editor explained to his team that I would be joining them for a few hours a week to learn about journalism and do some writing. I shook hands with Billy Spence, a long-serving reporter who had been writing sports reports in the town since the 1960s and was a legend in local circles. There was Neil Fullerton, a future sports editor at the *Daily Mirror*, Steven Alexander, who went on to work for the Alliance Party, Martin McKillop, who also went on to bigger publications, and Dessie's then deputy, Stephen Kernohan.

Struck with shyness for a few minutes, I remained silent as Dessie and Robert talked about my start date, which would be the following Tuesday.

As we drove back to the centre, Robert and I reflected on a successful encounter, and he urged me to make the most of this grand opportunity. He believed I had long-term potential for a regular column.

Little did I know that the following Tuesday would mark the start of an eighteen-year association with the *Ballymena Times*. Characteristically, I was more nervous than ten newborn kittens. I was desperate to impress. I was sitting exactly where I wanted to be. After years of saying that I was a reporter in waiting, it seemed like I dare not waste this chance. My early stories were NICOD related.

I will never forget my second week when Dessie and the crew returned from printing the paper in Portadown to present me with a copy of that day's edition. Turning to page five, my editor showed me a piece I had written about the first anniversary of the TORNEO project for people with acquired, traumatic brain injuries. Beneath the headline, which read 'TORNEO'S first year is a huge success' was By: Joe Boyd. My first by-line! If you had handed me one million crisp notes at that moment, I don't think I would have been more elated.

A few minutes later, a taxi arrived to take me back to NICOD. On arrival I rushed into Robert's office to show him. I think I might well have danced up the corridor. I felt like a real reporter. I had done it! Of course, I was only at the beginning of my journey. There would be hundred, if not thousands more 'By: Joe Boyd' tags to come, but I will never forget that first one or those who made it possible.

Although my early NICOD stories were well written and positively received, it must be said my breakthrough story in terms of gaining journalistic credibility emerged because of my connections to that sphere, albeit in very troubling circumstances.

One Wednesday night in November 1997, just months into my *Ballymena Times* apprenticeship, a gang of idiots broke into the grounds where Beechgrove and Dunfane Special Schools were situated. For some reason known only to themselves, they proceeded to smash several windows at both schools and those of minibuses parked there. They also damaged expensive computer equipment. This rampage occurred just a couple of months after the adventure playground at Beechgrove had been destroyed in an arson attack.

Infuriated after the second incident, I charged into work on Thursday morning, and Dessie gave me the opportunity to write an editorial comment column to be printed alongside the news coverage of the incident. In my comments, I informed our readers that the perpetrators of the attacks had not just 'smashed up a couple of ordinary minibuses' nor had a run-of-the-mill public playground been destroyed, but the lives of struggling children had been deeply affected. I went on to say that many of the pupils at Beechgrove 'struggled to walk, talk or even feed themselves without assistance'. For them, I told my audience, 'their school was one of the few places where they could have fun and enjoy themselves.' I concluded by addressing the people who were responsible for the vandalism:

You are good-for-nothing pathetic dirt and you are guilty of ruining the lives of little boys and girls who have enough difficulty in finding happiness. If your actions were undertaken for a dare or a bet, I hope that whatever you have won was worth it. If you did it just for a laugh, I hope you are happy and proud of yourself because no one else is.

The tone of my reflections divided the people who read them. Some were quick to pat me on the back and say: 'Spot on, Joe.' Others, my own mum included, were less positive: 'I suppose I have to be grateful you didn't use bad language,' intoned the Boyd matriarch. Someone from within my church said: 'We might have thought some of the things you said, but it wasn't appropriate to say it in a newspaper.'

From within the paper, however, all feedback was positive. Dessie said, 'If anything deserves to be read, that does.' Steven Alexander, another young reporter, told me a few months later that he rarely remembered anything that was written in a local newspaper, but that piece had stuck in his head. These comments were important to me, as I believed that to be a credible reporter, it was necessary to move beyond gentle NICOD-based or church-orientated copy, worthy as those stories may be.

In terms of my own thoughts about what I wrote regarding the vandalism incidents affecting Beechgrove and Dunfane, I have no regrets about my tone of the editorial. Whoever burned down the playground or smashed the windows knew exactly what they were doing when. The children who attended Beechgrove in the 1990s were more severely disabled that me and many of my contemporaries, so the area the thugs destroyed was a lifeline for those pupils. Whoever ruined it deserved to be condemned.

The same principle applies to any comment or news piece I have ever written. I have never knowingly lied to my readers, and any editorial piece I have ever compiled has been a true reflection of my thoughts at the time. Such honesty was and is part of my witness both as a Religious Affairs Correspondent and as a Christian.

Not all of the people I encountered during my time at NICOD/the Cedar Foundation or even the *Ballymena Times* were Christians. Even so, God used them to help me to grow, develop, and mature in preparation for the plans He had for me in later life

Preparations for my future accelerated as my teenage angst and frustrations receded. Little by little God opened more doors for me to grow spiritual and serve Him. In keeping with my limitations, the first opportunity He presented was very close to home.

CHAPTER EIGHTEEN

'WOULD YOU LIKE TO STAY WITH US?'

Finding My Place in the Christian Community

I had always enjoyed attending Boys' Brigade in the Connor Presbyterian Church. I liked being one of the older lads with responsibility for younger members. Going up to the BB's Northern Ireland headquarters in Larne for the weekend to work towards my Queen's Badge, the highest award given in the organisation, was a big adventure for me. I loved my weekly visits to a local residential nursing home for the elderly, where I undertook the Community Service element of my award. The residents valued having someone spend time with them, and it felt like a proper, important, grown-up thing to be doing, which fit in with how I wanted to be perceived.

At the end of that year in BB, I was awarded my Queen's Badge and the cup for Best Around Boy in the Company Section. I was absolutely thrilled and so was everyone around me. I loved seeing my picture in the newspaper and I was humbled to be described as 'an inspiration'.

I was even more delighted when, on the Monday night after the Display, the BB Captain asked me, 'Would you like to stay with us next year as a Staff Sergeant?'

I very quickly said yes, and that was the beginning of a career as a BB Officer, which lasted over fifteen years. I had special responsibility for the Recruits group, made up of the eleven-year-olds in their first year in the Company Section.

I grew into this role over time. I was by no means a natural leader, and for the first couple of years at least, I remained little more than an honorary older member of the Company rather than an authority figure. I was too focussed on getting the boys to respect the BB, as I wanted them to achieve and benefit as I had. I worshipped the organisation and its components rather than the God behind them. I was frustrated with boys who didn't try as hard with their badgework, drill, or games as I had done. I didn't mean them any harm; I was trying to impress and to do the job right. Unfortunately, I forgot that I had enjoyed BB so much because I was shown love, care, and compassion by leaders who tolerated my errors and loved me despite them. Truth be told, my early attempts at leadership probably put off more boys than I encouraged, and for that I am sorry. I was still growing up myself, desperate to please and be accepted.

In the years that followed, I realised that boys were not born for BB; rather, BB was established for boys. That helped me become a more compassionate youth worker. Certainly, by the time my legs got too old and I retired in 2012, I hope that I helped to advance Christ's kingdom among boys, just as the BB motto states.

God was also starting to use me at the *Ballymena Times*. Another of my early pieces was the interview with a missionary couple, Charlie and Flo Houston, who served with the Far-Eastern Broadcasting Association in the Seychelles. In my introductory paragraphs I wrote the following:

For most of us, the palm-tree fringed islands of the Seychelles exist only in a distant daydream. However, life on those sun-kissed islands has been a reality for Moorfields couple, Charlie and Flo Houston over the last nine years.

So delighted by my creativity was Dessie Blackadder that he rang the NICOD Centre to congratulate me on a great article about the Houston family. He also had told the editorial director at Morton Newspapers Head Office about my abilities. As you can imagine, I walked ten feet tall after that conversation!

Much of my time in the early days at the *Times*

was also spent telephoning local ministers, asking them to write for our 'Paper Pulpit' column, in which a different member of the local clergy wrote a 500-word sermon-style article for the Church News page. Persuading clergy to contribute to the press in those days was often difficult, as many of them still viewed the press with a degree of suspicion. Ever tenacious, I managed to pin someone down for an article most weeks. Their musings proved popular with our readers, who browsed our newssheet every week to see if 'their' minister had been selected. I recall being accosted by an elder from my own church who was very disappointed not to see a 'Paper Pulpit' in the edition he had purchased earlier that day.

Another feature I oversaw was the 'My Top Ten' column. In this, we asked someone to compile a list of their ten favourite songs and explain why he or she had chosen each one. Most of the charts I received were from people I knew, but I also managed to obtain the top ten music choices from local celebrities like Ken Reid, the Political Correspondent at Ulster Television, and his fellow colleagues, as well as presenters Paul Clark and Tina Campbell. Glasgow Rangers defender Colin Hendry sent a selection after a request from Karen Fullerton, our deputy editor, who knew I had a soft spot for the Scottish giants. Gold medal Olympic athlete Dame Mary Peters also talked tunes when I telephoned her.

For the first few years at the *Times*, my contributions were limited by my OU study commitments. Although

I was excited to write for the paper, my studies took priority. A desire to banish the slow to learn tag burned within me, and it would be extinguished only with an advanced certificate of academic achievement.

CHAPTER NINETEEN

'YOU HAVE ENORMOUS POTENTIAL ACADEMICALLY'

Exercising My Grey Cells in Higher Places

I spent an incredible amount of time on my OU studies. I often took my textbooks to NICOD with me, and with the exception of Boys' Brigade on a Monday night or morning worship at church on a Sunday, you would find me in my room reading from around 9 a.m. until 8 or 9 p.m. I stopped only for meals or when my head started to ache with fatigue.

On one occasion, a colleague from the *Times* asked if I wanted to go with him to meet Ally McCoist, the Rangers and Scotland striker. I loved football but politely declined, as I had a chapter of Falcoult, the social policy philosopher, to read. My family thought I was mad, but in my mind, I was doing what I had to do. I had a limited secondary education and no ability for administrative work, so my only chance to secure any sort of future was to pass my degree course. To this day, I believe God used the OU to guide me back to the purpose He had for my life. I give Him all the glory for guiding the decisions I made. I have no regrets about working as hard as I did.

Successfully completing the Social Science Foundation course gave me a measure of confidence academically. That said, it hadn't been easy. I then enrolled for my first level-two credits with a degree of trepidation. I worried that moving up the academic scale might be a bridge too far for me.

The tutorials for my chosen module D211 Social Problems and Social Welfare were held on the Coleraine Campus of the Ulster University once a month on Saturday mornings. It would have been too much of a physical struggle to travel alone by train, so Mum very kindly accompanied me on my journeys to university for several years. I am so grateful to her for this, and I would not otherwise have made it to my classes. She was, and is, a true woman of God, whom He commissioned as my mother to bless me on this and many other occasions.

Sensitive to my fears about embarking on post-foundation level study, God brought Jane Castles into my life. Jane was the full-time staff tutor in charge of the Health & Social Care Faculty at the OU in Ireland. Her main role was administrative, but she kept her hand in practically by teaching the D211

Social Science course.

White-haired, bespectacled, and in her mid-fifties, Jane initially struck me as someone who would be strict and officious. That first impression was dispelled after an hour when, during the first coffee break, I asked her to explain something I had not understood in class. When I failed to grasp her first explanation, she used another analogy I could better understand. I thanked her and apologised for asking the same question twice. Her response typified all her interactions with me from then until we last saw each other at my wedding nearly twenty years later. 'Joe, don't apologise. I don't care what question you ask me or how many times you ask. I will explain the answer to you until you understand it.'

She explained things to me in ways I could understand. She was incredibly patient and generous with her time. If I rang her, day or night, she always made time to speak with me. I rightly acknowledge Ethel Kenny as the person God used to spark everything in my mind, and fifteen years later, He brought Jane Castles alongside me to restore the abilities that six years in an unsuitable special secondary school had threatened to destroy.

Under Jane's direct tuition, my assignment marks went through the roof, as did my punctuation! Not only did Jane correct my use of apostrophes and commas, her academic feedback on every piece of work I submitted was so clear that improvement was easy.

Leaving aside her teaching ability, the most important things Jane gave me were her time, her counsel, and her friendship. She was excellent as my D211 tutor, and her feedback on my final TMA report stated that I had 'enormous potential academically.' She continued to counsel me throughout my degree and beyond.

In truth, her real impact on my work occurred when she was no longer my tutor. Despite my good marks in second year, including high scores for my written coursework, I merely scraped through my end-of-year exam with a low mark.

A bemused Jane contacted me at the start of the following term. 'Joe, we need to find out why you didn't do better in your exam.'

'But Jane, I did pass,' I mumbled.

'Yes, you did, but you scored seventy percent in your TMAs and only forty percent in the exam. You were very good in class, and yet you barely managed to scrap through. Did your revision go okay?'

'Yes, it did. I worked hard every night.'

'I know you did your best, and that is why we have to find out what is stopping you from getting the results someone of your ability should.' She suggested that I go for a course of self-hypnosis, which the university could fund on her recommendation—she could be quite persuasive. Mum and I travelled to Ballymoney for the sessions, which I enjoyed and found relaxing.

My third year ran in tandem with this therapy. I had chosen to read the K201 Working with Young

People course, which I enjoyed. My coursework marks remained high.

October arrived and with it my end-of-year exam date. Margaret Rodgers came to our house with the exam paper. She handed it to me, I took a deep breath, and . . . froze!

At one point, as I slowly typed a few words, desperately trying to get my brain to work, Margaret asked, ‘Are you stumped?’

I muttered something about just thinking, although I was just relieved when the three-hour period was over, and I was free to walk out. Christmas Eve arrived and with it a letter from the university stating that I had scored well in my coursework and 39 percent in my examination. I was granted a Grade 4 pass because of my written assessments.

Investigations into why someone who performed so ably throughout the year only to fall at the final hurdle continued. In year four, I selected a course on 20th Century America. As well as looking at US politics, these modules covered the history of rock music, art, and cultural life in the States. I really enjoyed this material, especially the chance to listen to Bill Haley, Little Richard, and Patsy Cline while studying. Again, my coursework marks were high.

Exam time arrived again, and the written test score was again below the required grade. This time, I was asked to attend an oral examination at the OU’s headquarters in Belfast. This was overseen by one of the OU’s professors from England. We spent an hour in conversation about the topics covered in the course while the Social Science Staff Tutor in Belfast, Dr Pat Jess, listened on. Eventually, the professor smiled. 'I think I have heard enough. I will make my report to the examiners, but, please, don't worry about it.' Pat Jess smiled broadly and gave me a warm pat on the back. She, too, was a great support to me.

The next day I spoke to Jane, whom Pat had told that 'there was no question about my knowledge of the course.' Sure enough, a few days later, a letter from the university arrived with the news that I had scored 83 percent in both my exam and my coursework. We were in business!

Always on the ball, Jane suggested that an amanuensis be appointed to see me through future examinations. In layman's terms, this describes someone who writes answers to exam questions as dictated by the test taker. Jane had come to realise that the physical stress of writing answers on exams caused my brain to shut down, rendering me incapable of reading and writing. She and Pat concluded that when I was able to speak my answers rather than write or type them, the physical stress disappeared, as it had during my oral test. Before my fifth year began, I moved up to Honours Level courses, but my marks remained in the 80s with two scores of 90-plus percent.

The amanuensis arrived at my home for the end-of-year test, only to leave a few hours later without the use of her right hand. I managed to produce about ten pages of written work. Christmas came, and with it news that I had scored 74 percent in my written exam. God was good, and I thanked Him accordingly.

My final year studies were based on the theme of Crime & Punishment. Jane believed I could achieve a 2:1 classification in my degree, though I still doubted my own ability. Could I, the boy whose intelligence was declared below normal, really graduate?

The final year work was tough. Though I did well in class, my coursework averaged in the low 70s, and I needed another 70-plus score to get my 2:1.

I was grateful to have Margaret, my former exam invigilator, with me as my notetaker. She was extremely accurate and very encouraging. On one occasion the tutor asked each class member to examine two pieces of work and then say which one would attain the highest mark. I spotted the answer immediately while everyone else struggled. As I went to raise my hand, Margaret whispered, 'You have analysed that quicker than anyone else. Don't make it easy for them by giving away the answer. Give them time to think it through.' I was beginning to understand how far I had come in knowledge and maturation to see that I didn't need to prove that I was as capable as my able-bodied classmates.

Going into the final exam, I was nervous. I would have to be on top of my game as I had averaged only about 72 percent in my coursework, and my test scores usually showed a slight drop. I couldn't afford that. I had to do better. I completed my paper. I wrote about twelve pages and knew I had passed, but would it be enough? All I could do now was wait.

December arrived and, at last, the final reckoning. I ripped open the envelope . . . 71 percent. I had done it! I hugged Granny and Mum. I rang Margaret, and Jane, who already knew, Robert from NICOD, and anyone else I could think of! I praised God, acknowledging that He was behind my success. The doctor's report from years before was consigned to history. I was Joseph Boyd BSc (Hons) Sol Pol (Open). Those hard-earned letters would never be taken from me. When God restores, He achieves spectacular results.

During my six years of OU study, I very deliberately set myself the challenge of reading a chapter from the Bible each night. I received my degree certificate around the same time that I finished reading the book of Revelation. Disciplining myself to get through a chapter each night after frying my brain with study was tough. But I look back on that as a key phase in the development of my walk with God. It is only because of Him that I was able to graduate. When I was messing about in my teens, I was a failure. The words of John 15:5 sum up my journey through my education, work, life, and, later love, perfectly: 'I am the vine; you are the branches. If you remain in me and I in you, you will bear much fruit; apart from me you can do nothing.'

I remember my graduation day from the OU with great fondness. Jane rugby-tackled me at the door, and I got a bear hug from Pat Jess. Mum, Dad, Mark, Megan, and Granny were there to see me graduate.

Jane led me up to the stage of the Waterfront Hall, depositing me into the arms of Baroness Boothroyd, ex-speaker of the House of Commons and OU Chancellor. Former Secretary of State for Northern Ireland, the late Mo Mowlam, was also on the platform to receive an honorary doctorate. Seeing what a huge physical effort I had made to get up on stage, both politicians put their arms round me, and we spent some time in conversation. They ensured that my day was memorable. Conversation over, I walked to the end of the platform to be collected by Jane, and we made our way back to our seats.

With letters firmly affixed after my name, I said good-bye to the OU but not to Jane. We remained close friends for the rest of her life. Though frail, she made it to my wedding. Her death occurred suddenly just a few weeks later. When her daughter rang to let me know that her mother had passed away, she said, 'Mum really enjoyed your wedding because you made a fuss of her.' Apparently, it was one of her final trips out, and I consider it an honour that she made such an effort for me. I give God all the glory for my educational achievements, but I believe that Jane was sent by the Lord as a guardian angel. I will never forget her.

With my degree finished, it was time to go to work. Thankfully, God already had me in place at the *Ballymena Times* and would begin to use me there consistently in some very significant ways.

CHAPTER TWENTY

'YOU'RE ONE OF THOSE PAPER BOYS, AREN'T YOU?'

The Place I Called Home

Writing regularly for a proper newspaper was the fulfilment of my dream. The achievement of my aspiration emerged as a gift from God, which I endeavoured to use for His glory. Unlike many things you wish for as a child, becoming a professional journalist has given me everything I hoped it would, and more. I praise my Saviour for His generosity and the many ways He has blessed me through journalism.

For many years prior to my arrival at the *Ballymena Times*, Jack Adams, a well-known local photographer and historian, covered the Churches News section. As the millennium turned, Jack became increasingly busy with his commitments to the local Historical

Society and Radio Cracker Ballymena, a charitable broadcasting organisation.

I had already written quite a lot of Christian material for the paper during my student years, so I was invited to take over the church-based section once I had secured my degree. This promotion was a God-given opportunity, for it gave me a worthwhile task to complete each week as well as a small income under the permitted work scheme, whereby people with disabilities can earn a little extra money while retaining their state benefits. Just as importantly, spending time at the newspaper gave me an avenue for social interaction both with the staff and with friends and acquaintances I made in the churches around Ballymena. I also grew to realise that if I was going to write about God in the newspaper, it was important to behave in a manner honouring to Him. Being a good witness became ever more important, and the Lord challenged me more and more about this as time progressed.

For example, I always went into the office in Tuesdays to start planning for the following week's column. Each week, the sports editor, Billy Spence would ask: 'Well Joe, did you go to church on Sunday?' If I replied no, he would ask why. The he'd inform me that he had left the office on Sunday morning in time for morning service at West Presbyterian in Ballymena, where he attended every Sunday, so there was no excuse for me to miss a service.

I have to say that Billy has been a great friend to

me over all the years I have known him. He spent time with me on Tuesday afternoons talking about the football and his beloved Liverpool FC. We bonded over a mutual dislike for Manchester United. Every year, Billy would also take my BB Week Appeal Card to Ballymena courthouse with him when he reported on the weekly cases that were heard there. He secured several generous donations from local solicitors. Dessie Blackadder and the other reporters also involved me in office life as much as they could, ensuring that I was invited to staff lunches and social occasions. The advertising team, affectionally known as 'the girls downstairs', also took me into their hearts. The Advertising Manager, Stephanie Manson, and her deputy, Lynda Gillen, were especially kind and frequently invited me to their departmental lunches, too. Lynda's sister, June, also worked in the paper and secured a surprise meet-and-greet for me with Jason Donovan when he performed a concert in Belfast. The photographers, Jim McCaw, John 'Curly' McIlwaine, and Alan McMullan, were also brilliant and ensured that I never had to walk too far up the street in Ballymena when they spotted me in town, even if I was 'off duty'.

I have included these reminiscences not for nostalgic reasons, rather because the time and affection given to me by all the staff at the *Ballymena Times* played an important part in my personal and spiritual growth. Being there gave me a legitimate network beyond home and church—a variety of people to speak to and interact with—and God sent me there for all these reasons as well the compilation of 'His' pages in the paper.

Dessie's positive response to my early piece about the missionary family who served in the Seychelles indicated my prowess as a Church News writer. Shortly after that piece, I wrote

another article about the long-serving organist at Kells Presbyterian Church who retired in 1997 after forty-one years behind the ivories. Soon afterwards, Rev Brian Boyd received a visit from his friend Alfoldly-Boruss Dezso, who pastored a congregation in the Hungarian Reformed Church. This gave me an opportunity to report that 'Kells Christians were "Hungary" for the faith.' The director of Child Evangelism Fellowship in my home area, Jonathan Reid, was a close family friend; therefore, during my early months at the paper, I had the privilege of interviewing CEF missionaries from Albania, Dublin, Norway, and Albania when they visited Ballymena. These articles were good confidence builders and helped me demonstrate there was more to me that just disability-related stories.

Any local reporter will probably tell you that the best scoops emerge from the most unlikely places. Believe it or not, I unearthed at least one front-page lead from a conversation with a taxi driver as he transported me to the office one morning.

'You're one of those reporter boys, aren't you?' the driver asked.

'Yes,' I replied.

'Do you report on anything?'

'Well, I am known as the Churches Correspondent, but, yes, I help with other things, too.'

'It's just that on Saturday night, I was driving in the car and my two-year-old granddaughter was in the back. Some young ones were throwing bits of brick at passing cars. One of them hit my side door. A foot higher and the wee one would have been killed or seriously hurt. Will you write that in your paper for me?'

I invited the driver to repeat his words into my tape recorder. A few minutes later, he dropped me off and I went in and told my colleagues what had happened. It turned out that several other people from the same area of the town had contacted the office to report similar incidents. A couple of days later, I picked up the latest edition of the *Times* the front-page headline read: 'Baby escapes brick attack' with my by-line under the story, which included a regurgitation of my conversation with the driver. What a result!

Although I was mainly a Church News correspondent, God allowed me to be in the right place at the right time for stories like this as a small reward for my work. He knew that I loved my Christian section but that I also harboured dreams of being acknowledged as a 'hard news' reporter—at least from time to time.

God was also with me when penned the saddest

story I ever had to write—an obituary to mark the passing of Ethel Kenny in 2003. She and I had stayed in regular contact over the years. During the last few years of her life, I rang her regularly for a chat or to ask advice. Writing the tribute piece to mark her death was, perhaps, the most gut-wrenching task I have undertaken as a journalist. I believe with all my heart that God put me in place to write the article and ultimately gave me the strength to compile it when I wanted to curl into a ball and weep with grief

Occasional forays into secular stories aside, I am remembered at the *Ballymena Times* for being 'the Churches Correspondent', a title I will proudly wear because I regularly helped to bring Christian news to a secular publication. It was an honour for me to meet and write about some of the best-known missionaries in the province. I spent time with Clare McIntyre, who taught in Malawi for many years under the auspices of the Presbyterian Church in Ireland. There was also Bobby and Tilly Toner from Ahoghill, a remarkable couple who spent most of their lives in Japan as pastors. I talked to Maisie Smyth, who served in the Democratic Republic of Congo for several decades, not to mention the lovely Mary Steele who worked in Bible Translation with Wycliffe for over sixty years and managed to translate the full Scriptures into both the Bimoba and Konkomba dialects. The amazing feature that stands out in each of these people was their humility despite their incredible achievements for the kingdom of God. When Mary Steele received her MBE for Services to Bible Translation in 2006, she wrote me a lovely note after reading my article.

Dear Joe,

Thank you for your article about my work with Wycliffe. It was very well written; only I felt uneasy about all that praise! I believe that all the glory belongs to God alone.

Many blessings,

Mary Steele

I also met and interviewed Rev Patricia Storey when she served her curacy in the Parish of Kilconriola and Ballyclug, which encompassed Ballymena. A quiet and genuine person, she later went on to become the first woman to serve as an Anglican Bishop in the UK and Ireland when became Bishop of Meath and County Kildare.

Throughout my newspaper years, one of my goals was to encourage Christians to see beyond the local church and its traditions, important as they were. While it was a pleasure to be writing about Harvest Services, Christmas events, and the opening of new church halls, I yearned to write articles about overseas mission work or the Christian-led efforts to combat addiction and prompt the church to meaningful social action.

Always keen to take me out of my sphere of comfort, God engineered an encounter that would take me from behind my desk and on to the streets of Ballymena in His service.

CHAPTER TWENTY-ONE

'HERE'S ONE FOR YOU, JOE'

A Spark-ling Place

In March 2007, I received a telephone call from Rick Hill. I had known him for several years, and he, along with several other young adults from around Ballymena and the neighbouring town of Antrim, had been involved in various street-based Christian outreach projects across Ireland.

Rick, in partnership with Matt Boyd, wanted to visit with me to get an article into the paper about an outreach project they were organising that upcoming summer in Ballymena called Spark (Servants Pursuing a Radical Kingdom).

Intrigued, I met with them and invited the young men to tell me about Spark and why they felt led to birth it.

Matt explained that both he and Rick had been

involved in Belfast Streetreach. At some stage during this, the two had 'got chatting' and decided that it would be a good idea to organise something similar in Ballymena. Matt lived in Ballymena and Rick, from Antrim, was a frequent visitor and knew the town well.

Matt and Rick went on to tell me that through Spark, they hoped to bring together Christians from all denominations who would act as 'Jesus's hands and feet' in Ballymena, showing His love to people in different areas of the town. With this aim at the fore, Spark would be active in seven parts of the town: Harryville, Doury Road, Dunclug, Ballykeel, Fisherwick, Ballee, and the town centre. Late-night cafés would be in operation, along with gardening teams, holiday Bible clubs, and various other community-based activities.

A Spark crew would be at Broadway Bandstand in the centre of town. Their job would be to hand out to passersby free tea, coffee, sweets, and worship CDs, while also being on hand to explain their mission and tell about Jesus. I had written about Rick and Matt's experiences as part of the Worship Ireland collective, which travelled across the island for a few summers in the mid-1990s, so their plans intrigued me.

I asked the lads to explain how any of our leaders who wanted to get involved could find out more. Rick reached into a folder and produced two application forms. 'There's one for under-eighteens,' he said. Then he pointed to another form for adults. As he did,

Rick winked at me. 'That's one you could fill in.'

I smiled as a little butterfly flitted in my stomach. 'Thank you very much.' Truthfully, that butterfly was actually the Holy Spirit stirring my soul.

Matt and Rick left soon afterwards. I sat at my desk to begin transcribing the interview from my tape recorder. The process was slowed because I couldn't stop looking at the blue application document Rick had given me. I must have read it through about five times in one afternoon.

As the day progressed, I texted two or three Christian friends, telling them about 'this outreach project that Worship Ireland were doing in Ballymena that summer.' I told them that I was thinking of getting involved and asked what they thought. Their responses were positive, with one person sounding particularly enthusiastic. 'Oh yeah, you should definitely go for it. Our church is getting involved as well.' From then on, I felt an urgency to fill out the form and post it. I took it home and showed it to Mum, who kindly filled in the page and sent it off that evening.

A few days later, I received a phone call from another of the Worship Ireland guys whom I had met several times through the paper. He asked if I would meet him for coffee in town. Gladly, I accepted the invitation and we met a few days later. Although the word *interview* was not actually used, I recognise an interview. My companion enquired about my background, testimony, and continuing walk with God. Answering his questions as honestly as I could, I shared a few horror stories about my teenage years, including the incidents of nastiness and violence towards my parents at the height of my problems. Listening sympathetically, the young man nodded and smiled. Coffee consumed, he explained that he had 'wanted to get to know the Joe behind the Dictaphone' and felt the meeting helped him do that. He then gave thanks for my life, witness, and deliverance from difficult circumstances before we said our good-byes, and I headed back to the office.

In the weeks that followed, I received occasional group texts from the Spark team, urging those who had already signed up to spread the word and pray for what lay ahead. I guessed that I had been accepted to be part of the summer's activities. Eventually, the phone bleeped with a message inviting Sparkers to a training day at Victory Praise Community Church in Ballymena. Nervously, I attended, still uncertain as to whether I, a twenty-eight-year-old man who used a wheelchair and spent his days writing church notes for the local paper, had anything to offer these vibrant and talented young Christians with whom I was surrounded. Nevertheless, I was happy to let my application stand and see what happened. I thought my participation in Spark would be a one-off blessing from God, who was graciously allowing me to enjoy the kind of summer mission team experience I had missed out on as a messed-up teenager. I anticipated that I would go along for the week, have a reasonable time, and then go back to my life, happy to have ticked the 'I have taken part in a summer team' box.

Little did I know that from the moment I stepped into the over-eighteens meeting on the first Saturday of Spark 2007 that the project would grab my heart to the point where, as I write in 2018, I am one of only a handful of the original group who were present when the project began. From the first worship session at High Kirk Presbyterian Church on the inaugural Monday morning, I knew I was exactly where God wanted me to be. I was happy to do this.

Proof, if any were needed, that God has a sense of humour was evidenced by the fact that He took me away from work for a week on a missionary experience only to plant my wheelchair directly across the road from the *Ballymena Times* office! The nice thing about that was seeing many of my colleagues from the paper come over to the bandstand to visit me and receive a CD. I had an opportunity to explain what I was doing and why. That was another reminder from the Lord about the importance of maintaining a genuine Christian witness at work and at home. Had I not been living a consistent and open Christian life at work, giving out music and talking about God to passersby would have made me a hypocrite.

It never ceases to amaze me how giving someone a CD, a tract, or a cup of coffee can provoke such a range of reactions. Some people simply said, 'No, thank you', or even less as they walked past. Others took one and moved on. A few chuffed at receiving something without having to pay for it. My stock reply was, 'All of this is free because God's love is free.' Occasionally, the freebies offer an opportunity to start deeper conversations about God with individuals who reveal deeply personal aspects of their lives.

As a leader on the project, I continue to be blown-away by how well younger Spark volunteers, some aged thirteen or fourteen years old were able to answer deep spiritual questions often posed to them by much older adults who were hostile to the gospel or what we are doing.

One man accosted me on the bandstand and tried to tell me that what we were doing at Spark was not Christian outreach but merely a form of street entertainment.

'But these young people are Christians who want to serve the Lord, and this is how they express their love for Him.' I said. 'What should I be doing with them?'

'Tell them to go home and obey their parents,' he said.

Before I could utter a retort, a young team member came up to the man and said, 'I am here because I love God and I know that He loves me. The Bible tells us to go out into all the world and spread the good news.'

The gentleman walked away.

Personally, I learned more from Spark and its young volunteers than I ever gave them. I enjoyed building friendships, having fun, and eating the lovely meals cooked for us by the churches each year. More importantly, I have grown to understand that it is not possible to be the complete answer to everyone's problems. We can simply point them in the right direction.

During the project's first year, I spoke to a man who was an alcoholic and had been evicted by a government-run housing scheme thirteen times. He wanted me to find him somewhere to sleep. Another older team member and I took him out for fish and chips and listened to his story. He wanted us to provide him with a house to stay in, so we pointed him in the direction of the YMCA, who could provide temporary accommodation. Sometimes in situations like this, I wished we could have done more; however, we always did the best we could.

I have also come to understand that outreaches where young people are involved work best when their needs are taken into consideration and catered for. Sometimes in the past I have been guilty of focussing so much on running an event that I have forgot the needs of the volunteers who are working the event. Spark teams have worked through rain, hail, and shine, and it is good for the young people to understand that serving Jesus involves sacrifice and can be inconvenient. However, sometimes, due to incremental weather conditions, we have had to cancel our plans and instead have gathered in the nearest coffee shop for a hot drink and an opportunity to build relationships with one another. In doing this, my hope is that those I am leading will recognise the importance of leading with compassion as I believe Jesus did.

I also love watching the young Spark volunteers grow into spiritually mature young men and women of God. Nothing is more rewarding for me than watching a shy, nervous thirteen-year-old become a confident twenty-something, leading alongside me with assurance about who he or she is in Jesus. I am delighted that many of the young people who have taken part in the project over the years have gone on to become pastors or youth workers or are serving in other ways. Of course, some have struggled in their faith. This is sad, but I firmly believe that the sheep know their Master's voice, and we have the promise in Luke 10:1–6 that God will continue to seek those who have lost their way and bring them back safely into His kingdom. I know this to be true from personal experience.

Spark continues to be active in Ballymena and has now spread to Newtonabbey. Overall leadership has passed from Matt and Rick to Lisa Jackson, a wonderful young woman. She continues to do a remarkable job. I will continue to support her for as long as God enables me.

Although I loved my work at the *Ballymena Times*, not every experience left me with such pleasant memories. Life brings both joys and disappointments. One difficult occasion will live long in my memory—for all the wrong reasons.

CHAPTER TWENTY-TWO

SHAKIN' WITH EMBARRASSMENT

'Right Place, Wrong Time'

Wednesday, 5 December 2009, I, along with my mum, an aunt, and hundreds of others, stood outside a Ballymena hotel on a snowy evening waiting to see '80s popstar Shakin' Stevens in concert.

I had always been a massive fan. As I mentioned earlier, Shaky's music helped me to walk and encouraged me through some of the toughest periods of my life. Now I was about to see Wales's answer to Elvis on stage in my hometown, and a colleague at the *Ballymena Times* had arranged a meet-and-greet with Shaky for me. What could go wrong?

For a start, the room in which the concert was to be held was not ready, much to the frustration of the audience who were standing out in freezing temperatures. Mr. Stevens was likely also frustrated. As result of the delay, a representative of the company in charge of promoting the event told me that my audience with Shaky would be delayed until after the concert.

Fair enough. It will be a late night, but I've been looking forward to this. I will enjoy the gig and see him later.

Finally, the audience filed in, eventually the lights went down, and Shaky appeared on stage to strains of 'Don't She Look Good?' This was a song from his *Shaky* LP, which was released in 1981. I sang my heart out.

At around halfway through the first segment of the evening, the freelance photographer on duty for the *Ballymena Times* entered the room. I had explained to him in a telephone call earlier that the photo of Shaky and myself would not be taken until after the concert but that he could get some shots of the artist performing on stage while someone else snapped my picture later.

As I understood it, security personnel at the show gave this same assurance to the lensman, so he believed, as did I, that he was well within his rights to take photographs during the performance.

At one point during the concert, Shakin' Stevens lifted a large microphone stand and walked towards my colleague. I assumed he was positioning himself to give the cameraman a great action shot. Then the singer appeared to make a sweeping movement towards the photographer, who quickly disappeared.

That was slightly odd. However, I was enjoying the gig, so I put it to the back of my mind. During the interval, I heard other audience members express surprise at Shaky's actions. 'The guy hasn't had a hit for twenty years. You'd think he'd be glad to have his photo taken.'

At this point, I began to worry that something was awry, and I felt guilty for the photographer and my newspaper colleagues. Knowing how much I enjoyed the crooner's music, a lot of effort had gone into arranging the photo shoot and meeting. I really didn't want to see anyone get hurt or for any bad feeling to linger.

The concert ended and the lucky few who had been granted access to Shakin' Stevens waited for our opportunity to meet the singer, which came about an hour later.

When we spoke, Shaky was as nice to me, as he had been when I interviewed him by telephone for an article promoting the concert. We spoke about his favourite music, and he congratulated me on the piece I had written about him. Once again, he complimented me on being able to walk well and said that he was pleased to have helped with that.

I left with a smile on my face, thinking that maybe the night had gone well after all.

Any illusions I had on that score where dispelled the next day when the photographer who had attended the concert telephoned me and asked for the promoter's details. His camera had been damaged by Shakin' Stevens when he moved the mike stand towards him. Not only that, he had also been injured in the incident. I gave the photographer the details he requested, hoping that I had heard the last of the whole affair.

Unfortunately, a couple of days later, I received a phone call from local police informing me that an allegation of assault and criminal damage had been made by the photographer against Shakin' Stevens, and that my name had been given as a witness. I arranged to give a statement to the police at the *Ballymena Times* office the following day.

In this, I stated what I believed to be the truth. I was seated about three rows back from the front and saw the photographer at the side of the stage. I had seen Stevens move towards the photojournalist and make a sweeping movement towards him, who moved away quickly. I informed the officer that the room was dark and that I couldn't say definitively whether the performer had connected with the camera or the photographer.

I maintained this testimony when the case went to court, and I, my mother, and my aunt were called as witnesses for the prosecution, along with some others who were present on the night of the concert.

I am ashamed to say that Stevens' barrister made mincemeat out of me in the witness box, pointing out that I had recorded a positive interview with the artist and even wrote to thank his fan club for helping to organise it. The television news coverage that night described how 'one witness crumbled during cross-examination when questioned about events on the night.' I am certain the report was referring to my testimony.

As you can imagine, other media outlets across the province, including television and radio news programmes, covered the case. I got a shock when I heard my name mentioned in connection with the matter in BBC Radio Ulster's *Talkback* programme. Predictably, our rival newspaper in Ballymena featured the story in delicious detail. The opposition newssheet devoted around half a page to my inept and stuttering testimony. I was mildly embarrassed, of course, but I realised that, as a writer for an opposing publication, I was fair game. In all honesty, I would probably have been just as gleeful if the tables had been turned.

Anyway, the case lasted two days. The judge ruled in favour of the photographer. Relieved, Mum and I left the courthouse.

Aggrieved by the verdict, Shakin' Stevens appealed, and everyone returned to the dock eighteen months later for Round Two.

I acquitted myself better in the witness box the second time around, even forcing a smile from the defending barrister as I anticipated his words. I did, however, feel a little sad as I caught a glimpse of Shakin' Stevens from across the room. Never did I imagine that I would ever be testifying against him.

Our meeting was supposed to be the fulfilment of a happy childhood wish.

Ultimately, his conviction was quashed on appeal, and so ended the most embarrassing chapter of my career. The outcome is a matter of record, and I will not question it here. I have known this photographer for many years, and I do not believe he would have instigated a case unless he felt he had grounds to do so. I also respect the right of Shakin' Stevens to appeal if he felt it was the correct course of action to take.

I look back on the situation with a degree of sadness, not just because my meeting with a hero was soured, but also because the incident need not have happened. If you set yourself up as a public figure, you open yourself to scrutiny. If you perform on a stage, you must expect your photo will be taken. Shakin' Stevens said that he blocked the photo as didn't agree to have his picture taken and was concerned to protect his 'image rights'. If violation of privacy worried him, he should not, in my view, have stood before four hundred people to sing.

But the questions is, what did I do for God through this episode? What did He want me to learn?

Perhaps, a jokey comment made by a minister had more to offer on the situation. 'You see, Joe, Shakin' Stevens was an idol in your life who needed to be torn down.'

The Bible says, 'You shall have no other gods before me' (Exodus 20:3). Perhaps my desire to meet Shaky for such a long had led me to worship the vessel God had used to encourage me to walk rather than the One who had got me to me feet. Making Shaky into a personal idol was unacceptable and had to change.

After all, 'Every good and perfect give comes from [God]' (James 1:17), and I include my ability to put one foot past the other as one of those gifts. All the glory for everything I can do belongs to the Lord alone.

If the only painful moment I ever had to endure in life was a run-in with Shakin' Stevens, I am a very blessed man indeed. However, when you have cerebral palsy or any physical disability you are no stranger to aches, pains, and various limitations. The fact that God has turned these negatives to positives offers a mind-blowing demonstration of His power and generous nature in which He works to bring good things into my life.

CHAPTER TWENTY-THREE

MADE IN GOD'S IMAGE

'Accepting My Place'

The Lord does not cause anyone to have a disability or illness. Genesis 1:31 says, 'God saw all that he had made, and it was very good.' The existence of disability in this world in all its forms occurred only after what is described in Genesis 3 as the fall, which is when humanity decided to make a dent in a previously perfect world by disobeying God. Because of man's rebellion against God, all the terrible things that we now see and experience on this planet (e.g., decay, ageing, sin, and disability) came into being.

Disability and illness come from God's enemy, the devil, who specialises in misery and suffering. He is described as 'the father of lies' (John 8:44). God, on the other hand, is the giver of 'life, and have it to the full' (10:10). God did not intend for disability to be part of the equation; it is the devil's doing. The question of why God, who is infinitely more powerful than the devil, allows disability is a thorny one, and an ill-judged answer is liable to cause offence. I do not know exactly why I have been allowed to have a disability, nor do I know why my condition is more or less severe than another's.

Honestly, my physical disability has impacted my life, both physically and cognitively, in ways that, at times, I truly wish it hadn't. It took me until mid-adulthood to come to terms with the fact that cerebral palsy prevents me from doing many things I would love to do.

For example, at numerous stages in my life, not being able to drive caused me immense frustration. I am not able to operate a car because the area of my brain which controls visual and spatial awareness is damaged so that I cannot safely judge distance, the position of other traffic, or safely steer a vehicle. On two occasions I attempted to defy the odds and learn to drive. The first time was at age seventeen. I was told very quickly that driving a car was impossible for me. The second attempt was just after I had finished my Ulster University counselling course. I had graduated twice although others said I was 'slow to learn'. I thought that just as I had bulldozed my way through university, I could get behind the wheel and succeed by hook or by crook.

With this attitude I began what turned into five

years of weekly driving lessons with Disability Action and three attempts at the driving test—with at least thirty-five major faults on each occasion. I had my 'good days' when lessons went well, but I could never sustain it. Mum, Dad, and others pleaded with me to surrender the aspiration when they noted how much the lessons took out of me both physically and emotionally.

Joye Carson, a good friend of mine, who was also prevented from driving because of poor eyesight, said, 'I think you want this for yourself more that the Lord wants it for you.'

In the end, my boss, Dessie Blackadder, ushered me into his office after my third attempt at the test and said, 'Son, I have known you and watched you for over ten years. In my opinion, no responsible Ministry of Transport official will ever award you a driving licence, and even if they did, it would come with no many conditions attached that it would not be worth having. I respect you, your degrees, and your writing ability, but you suffer too much pain and have too many weak moments to safely control a car. One lapse for a second could cause an accident and you would feel terrible.'

Dessie's words may sound harsh, but having worked under his editorial direction for years and known his compassion as a boss and a man, his words came from a place of concern. They were the catalyst for my decision to abandon this particular ambition.

Arguably, the most extreme battles I have fought

have been in my mind. A school of thought within cerebral palsy research proports the view that children with a purely physical disability are more likely to suffer from depression and low self-esteem due to an overwhelming ambition to match their able-bodied peers in every way. This is a feat that proves impossible, and, consequently, the young person's sense of self-worth is negatively impacted. Another professional I once encountered said that some individuals with cerebral palsy experience lower moods because their damaged brains are unable to produce dopamine at the same rate as cerebellums without injury.

Another theory that may go some way to revealing the reason behind my personal joust with mind games emerged during a course of prayer ministry about a year ago. I told the team praying for me about the difficult nature of my birth, and they suggested that my mind may have been impacted by the trauma that marked my entry into the world. This, they suggested, may have left its mark on me in the form of a mind prone to fear and turbulence.

A member of the team reminded me of Ephesians 6:12, which says, 'For our struggle is not against flesh and blood, but against the rulers, against the authorities, against the powers of this dark world and against the spiritual forces of evil in the heavenly realms.'

Another friend of mine, Willis McDowell, who later became my pastor, said this when I confided it him about my anxiety: 'Joe, you write the Christian page of the *Ballymena Times*, you lead in Spark and Boys' Brigade and many other things, while telling everyone that you love Jesus. Do you think that the devil is happy to let you do that? I don't think so. Satan will try to attack you where he thinks you are weakest. In your case, he makes you try to worry and doubt yourself, but he is a liar.'

Each of these ideas offer valid reasons in the search for an explanation as to why my mind plays the tricks it has done throughout my life. At Beechgrove School, I was recognised as a 'very nervous' child who was eager to please and feared doing anything wrong. Many years ago, I accidently erased the programme from a floppy disc on my computer. I worried for weeks that Mrs. Kenny would be cross. Of course, she wasn't. The software was reloaded. Problem solved. However, I believed I had done a terrible thing and that the consequences would be horrendous. My concerns dominated my every thought until I confessed what had happened.

In secondary school, my teachers told Mum and Dad that I was 'anxious all the time.' In my teenage years, my low moods caused me to become incredibly fearful. I have already recalled when I sat in the caravan in Portrush pretending that I wanted to watch cricket, when, in truth, I didn't want to meet anyone I knew, especially from school or outside the family.

At university, sheer panic overwhelmed me in

exams that rendered me unable to perform was another indication that something wasn't right in my mind.

The last sustained bout of anxiety occurred around a few years ago before my wedding. I am confident that I was not worried about marrying Rachael, as she feared. Indeed, I couldn't wait to make her Mrs. Boyd. My apprehension occurred, in part, because of the physiological or psychological cycle of depression/ anxiety that has been a consistent presence in my life.

I became very distressed by a role I had taken on as Company Secretary of a voluntary organisation. Once the fear took hold of my mind, it touched every area of my life. First, I struggled to accept affection from Rachael, then I worried that she would get tired of me and I would lose her love. This would, I reasoned, be a terrible failure on my part—proof that I was useless. It got to the stage where my head was so heavy and full of condemning voices telling me how rubbish I was that I became physically sore. Pain, pain, pain. Noise, noise, and more noise ringing constantly in my ears.

One Sunday morning I sat in my pew at Kells Church, my head buzzing with these horrible emotions. Thought creeped into my mind about going to the top balcony of the nearest tall building and jumping from it to my death. I reasoned that if I did this, the pain would stop and at least I would die in a place where I found some happiness.

This idea rolled around in my head throughout the

service. Then I looked round and made eye contact with Maggie, a close friend. The distress must have been etched on my face, for she beckoned me to her. I wrapped my arms around her for a prolonged hug. I can't remember exactly what I said to her, but throughout the afternoon, the crushing pain in my mind continued. I texted Maggie, asking her to pray. She returned for evening service. Having obtained my permission, she discreetly sought out Brian, the minister, and told him that all was not well with me.

Brian was extremely empathetic and sympathetic to my plight. He arranged to meet me a few days later. He assured me that I was not undergoing punishment from God, nor was I a 'bad Christian' for feeling as I did. We prayed together, and he confirmed that we could talk again anytime I needed. He also affirmed my plan to visit my GP to talk about how I was feeling and to seek help.

My own doctors were, as Brian and Maggie had been, very understanding. They arranged for me to attend counselling sessions and prescribe medication. Eventually, they diagnosed an anxiety disorder. After trying and discarding a few different medications, we found one that has made a real difference to my life. I still have occasional bad days, but I no longer wake up wishing every day was my last, nor do a fantasise about ending my life early to get to heaven, where there is no pain, suffering, or tears.

While I have accepted my disability, if a wonder drug were to come on the market that alleviated the symptoms of cerebral palsy with no side effects, I would gladly take it. Furthermore, I have undergone several surgeries, endured physiotherapy, and take medication daily. All these treatments have been useful and have enhanced my life.

All things are possible for God. He could cure my CP if He chooses to, but it is highly unlikely He will. Therefore, I must not only exist, but, more than that, live my life, enjoy it, celebrate it, cherish every aspect of it, roll with the punches, and say thank you daily for the opportunities I have.

One of the blessings that has helped me to look more positively to the future than ever before emerged arrived with a certain lady. God blessed me with Rachael, who has changed my life in an amazing way.

CHAPTER TWENTY-FOUR

'I KNOW SOMEONE YOU WOULD LIKE'

Putting My Heart in the Right Place

Rachael Warnock came into my life late spring or early summer 2012. I had met and dated a few women, but for various reasons those relationships had not worked out. Finding someone to spend my life with was another dream I hoped to accomplish.

As I approached my late thirties, I began to wonder if 'the one' really was out there for me. Slightly cynical after a couple of failed partnerships, I was sceptical when a friend of mine, Mandy Clarke, uttered, 'I know someone you would like.'

'Really, Mandy?' I said.

'Yes. She is a beautiful person, she doesn't live

far from you, and she drives. So you can spend time getting to know each other outside.'

At around the same time, Mandy must have had a similar conversation with Rachael about me. Both of us enjoy using Facebook, which provided an avenue for us to begin 'talking' with limited expectation on both sides.

Over a period of two or three months, I increasingly looked forward to exchanging messages with Rachael. We were both quite shy about meeting each other, and when I asked Rachael if she would like to meet me for a cup of tea or coffee, she said that she drank neither, which is actually true!

I noted how generous Rachael was even before we met. When I messaged her on Facebook that I was participating in a burger eating contest in support of Marie Cure Cancer Care, she promised to donate £10 in support of my efforts. The following Tuesday when I arrived at the *Ballymena Times* office for my shift, the receptionist gave me at envelope containing a £10 note, which Rachael had left for me.

Eventually, I think to shut me up more than anything, she promised to visit me some afternoon when I was on Broadway Bandstand during Spark week. True to her word, Rachael appeared with her niece, Olivia. We exchanged a brief hello before she headed back to the shops.

It took three or four months for us to meet properly. Mum and I were travelling to Yorkshire by boat for a short break while Rachael and one of her colleagues were on the same ferry taking some severely disabled adults on holiday to Blackpool as part of her work. During the voyage, her tenderness as she dealt with the severely disabled men who were mentally little more than children struck me. As one who has received care at various points in my own life, I can tell a lot about someone from how they treat others less able than themselves. Compassion cannot be faked. I knew then that Rachael was someone special and worth getting to know.

Upon our return home, our online chats became warmer and more personal. We shared more about our families, friends, and circumstances. Soon afterwards, we met for a meal together. We prayed before we ate. Once again, I was stuck by her warmth and gentleness.

We met for a breakfast, followed by a trip to the cinema the next Saturday, and yet more food. By now our texts and phone calls were daily. We enjoyed each other's company immensely.

Rachael became a regular visitor to the charity shop where I worked a few hours after finishing my newspaper articles each Friday. By October 2012, we both realised that we were more than friends. We had managed to secure tickets to a Graham Kendrick concert in Belfast, and as we strolled along the street following a pleasant meal, I asked permission to hold her hand. She agreed.

Although we got lost on our way to the concert, we had a lovely evening. We ended our time together with a gentle kiss. The rest, as they say, is history.

I began to attend Rachael's church, Victory Praise Community Church, on Sunday evenings. I knew some of the people who attended, and everyone was very warm and welcoming towards me.

We got to know each other's families. My parents liked Rachael instantly. She had a particularly soft spot for my father. I spent time with Rachael and her mum, Olive, at their home, just a short drive from my parents' house. On Fridays after finishing my shift at the charity shop, we visited Rachael's dad. Sydney lived in a nursing home as he was in the advanced stages of vascular dementia. I am so glad I was able to meet Rachael's father before he passed away. Even then, I believe he knew who we were. Walking into his room with Rachael one day, he remarked that I had 'nice glasses.' That moment has stuck in my mind to this day and is one of my favourite memories of Sydney.

I grew to deeply love Olive, and we spent a lot of time together in the final few years of her life. She was a staunchly Christian woman in her mid-70s. She read her King James Bible for up to four hours a day and spent more time in prayer than anyone I have ever known. Sometimes I used to watch her speak to the Lord in silence, hands clasped and eyes tightly shut. One could sense the Spirit of God resting upon her as she communed with her Saviour. It was almost tangible.

***

I am very blessed to be able to highlight the moment when I knew that Rachael and I were 'forever.' We were at a New Year's Eve Watchnight service at Victory Praise on 31 December 2012. Whether by divine province or sheer good fortune, Mandy Clarke had joined us at the gathering. Rachael had moved to another part of the room to speak to someone, and out of the corner of my eye I saw the warmest, most genuine smile break out across her face as she spoke to a child. At that point I whispered to Mandy, 'Do you think it is too early to ask Rachael to marry me?' Mandy simply smiled.

From then on, I was desperate to marry Rachael. With a fair degree of difficulty, I managed to wait until June 2013 to ask for Rachael's hand. I booked a short break for us at a hotel in rural Donegal. I had chosen and purchased a diamond cluster ring the previous week and grew more desperate to give it to the girl I loved. We travelled to Donegal on 4 June 2013. Before embarking on our main journey, we stopped off at Sydney's nursing home. We got to his room and Rachael remembered that she had left something for her father in the car. She disappeared, leaving Sydney and me in the company of a superb middle-aged caregiver who had a real heart for looking after elderly people. I turned to Sydney. 'Please, may I have permission to marry your youngest daughter?'

The carer became excited and urged her patient. 'Oh, go on, Sydney. Say yes.' She cajoled poor Sydney into uttering that magic word. The grin on the caregiver's face had grown as wide as the Atlantic Ocean by the time Racheal re-entered the room.

'Bye, bye, Daddy. I am going to Donegal with Joe for a few days. I will see you when I get back.' She sealed her promise with a kiss on her father's cheek.

'Have a lovely time!' The caregiver beamed, unable to keep the smile from her face.

'She was in good form this morning,' Rachael remarked as we walked back to the car.

I nodded. 'She was, indeed.' I smiled, though nervous.

The car journey to Donegal was one of the longest treks ever. Though lovely, our hotel turned out to be situated in one of the most remote locations on our island. Becoming ever more nervous, I remained silent for much of the drive, so much so that my soon-to-be fiancée asked, 'Why are you in such a bad mood? This is going to be a great few days.'

My stomach was doing somersaults with fear at the surprise question I was planning to ask her.

Being a romantic at heart, I had very grand plans for the proposal. I was all set to escort my beloved to the sandy beach opposite of our hotel for a long walk, end with a Clark Gable–esque declaration of love, followed by the all-important 'Rachael, will you marry me?'

As you can imagine, with a nervous wreck like me at the helm, things didn't work out as I planned. Rachael carried our bags up to the rooms we had booked. As her back was turned, I took the engagement ring out of my holdall and jabbered nervously. 'That's for you, my love' as I handed her the box.

'What is it?' Rachael enquired, lifting the lid.

Nerves froze my mind, because I can't remember what happened next. Rachael slipped the ring onto her finger and we hugged, so I presume we became engaged at that moment. Although, to this day, Rachael insists that at no point did she say yes to my 'proposal'!

We spent the next two days enjoying each other's company and being blissfully happy. The homeward journey didn't seem as lengthy as the trip coming, but we were both incredibly nervous about telling our families our news. We stopped off at a local restaurant for something to eat—only the swarm of butterflies in our tummies prohibited us from eating even a bite of food. Both plates returned to the kitchen untouched!

Rachael dropped me back to my parents' house while she went off to tell her own family.

'Nice time?' Mum enquired as I walked into the kitchen. She and Dad were sitting at the table.

'Very nice,' I replied. 'Eh, I asked Rachael to marry me.' I blurted the words.

'Does this mean you are engaged?' Mum asked.

'Yes.'

'That's wonderful!'

Dad shook my hand.

At that point, I rang Rachael, who was en route to her own mother and family.

Word quickly spread of the happy news, and we

began to plan our wedding. We set the date for 23 October 2014, exactly two years after our first kiss.

The day itself was wonderful, although it took every single second of fourteen months to plan. Rachael has a real love of children and has looked after many over the years. She had assured the many little girls who spent time with her that they would be her bridesmaids when she eventually tied the knot. Even though some of those girls were now adults, Rachael was determined to keep her word. As a result, she had eleven bridesmaids! I didn't mind a bit. Indeed, her generosity and belief that breaking this long-held promise would represent a bad witness to them was proof that I was marrying the right girl.

Our 140 or so guests shared our special day with us, which began with a service at Victory Praise, where we were married by the then pastor Willis McDowell. I was delighted that my own minister, Brian, also agreed to take part.

My wife looked stunning as queen of her entourage. Photos in a local beauty spot were followed by a wonderful reception at a golf resort and hotel about thirty minutes outside Ballymena. The function room was organised in the style of a sweetshop on the instruction of Rachael's best friend and matron of honour, Lorna, and her other close pal, Hester. These two remarkable ladies made sure that every aspect of the day was perfect for us.

Many guests told us that it was the nicest wedding they had ever been to. I suppose it would be difficult for them to say anything else. I wish I could go back in time to experience the day properly. Most things relating to it are a blur in my mind. I do remember making a point of greeting Jane Castles at the door, as she was frail and it took a big effort for her to attend. I enjoyed watching Rachael's delight at getting to share our special day with her friend, Irene, who lives in America.

Of course, I was nervous as I stood at the front of the church, desperate to catch the first glimpse of Rachael as she walked up the aisle on the arm of her brother, Stephen, who was giving her away. The exchange of rings was another memorable moment, simply because my hand was shaking so fiercely that I couldn't get the wedding ring fully onto Rachael's finger.

I cannot remember too much about my after-dinner speech. I do however recollect our first dance. I had trained for this in the gym for weeks beforehand under the supervision of my close friend and personal trainer, Aaron Benton. As one of my groomsmen, he was there to see all those balance and stability exercises pay off. A triumphant end to the best day of my life.

About a week later, Rachael and I set off for our honeymoon in Marrakesh, paid for by my parents. We found the country to be an array of contrasts. Nowhere was this more clearly demonstrated than in the disparity between 'old town' and 'new town' Marrakesh. One contained all the shopping malls, burger chains, while the other was like a scene from biblical Jerusalem. Camels plodded alongside people on worn dirt tracks. The poverty experienced particularly by mothers and children who lived on the streets were evident in their genuine hunger—they devoured in seconds any food we gave them.

A fortnight later, we returned home to settle into married life. Rachael returned to work as the main breadwinner while I stayed at home writing my newspaper column and looking after my mum-in-law, Olive.

I was delighted to have married the girl of my dreams, the one whom I loved with all my heart and continue to this day. She would never again leave my side at night, and that pleased me greatly. The only difficult aspect of my new life was having to say good-bye to Kells Presbyterian Church as my regular place of worship.

I made the decision to move to Victory Praise full time with Rachael as it was only a five-minute journey to VPC from our home, and I had known the pastor and others in the church for years. Leaving my home congregation behind was extremely painful for me. I loved and was loved by everyone there. I had served on the Congregational Committee, the Sunday school, Christian Endeavour and was a regular at every event that ran there. Rev Brian was a father-figure to me, and most of my friends worshipped there. Personally, I had known nothing but love, kindness, and unconditional acceptance from the people there, even through my troubled teenage years. Everyone was, and still is, very special to me. On my final Sunday, just four days before my wedding, I made the quickest possible exit, fearing I would cry if I hung around too long.

Victory Praise has brought new friends, and I love teaching in the Youth Bible Class and being part of the Cavetime Men's Group as well as the Clubreach team. It, too, is a special place where the Spirit of God dwells with sincerity and truth.

Married life, of course, brings challenges. Operating one's own house means bearing responsibility for things I used to leave to Mum and Dad. Racheal, as my wife, has first call on my time and energy. Loving your spouse as 'Christ loved the church and gave himself up for it' (Ephesians 5:25) takes time, effort, and commitment.

Add into the mix that we began married life as caregivers to Rachael's mum, who remained with us in the home. I would be lying if I said this did not bring challenges as well as joys. My abiding memories of my 'Queen Mum' Olive are happy ones. I spent many an afternoon listening to her stories about growing up in Omagh with her cherished family and friends. I consider it a privilege to have had this time with my wife's mother. Her death in August 2017 left a huge hole in our world. Even now, I miss being 'Boyd the Butler' to 'Lady Olive Shannon-Warnock'. She frequently scolded me over this posh pet name, although Rachael believes that her mum secretly enjoyed the sparring!

In truth, not a day goes by that I do not praise God for my darling Rachael and everything we have shared and, God willing, will share together. I am indeed blessed.

Spending time together is key, but I also believe that one of the secrets to sustaining a healthy marriage is for both partners to have legitimate, separate interests outside of the relationship. God has certainly been very gracious to me in the provision of some exciting, unexpected, and, given my physical status, some unconventional opportunities outside of our home.

CHAPTER TWENTY-FIVE

'AN INCREDIBLE FEAT'

A Challenging Place

In 2014, I began to volunteer three mornings a week at Pure Wellness gym, which is run by Green Pastures Church in Ballymena.

I had been a member of the gym since early 2012, when I noticed increasing stiffness in my body. Perhaps more importantly that, despite my busyness with writing and church, I was spending too much time alone or working. Although I knew a lot of people, I met with them in connection with either my role at the newspaper or while serving at church. While I enjoyed these activities, I felt lonely on a personal level. I needed a leisure interest outside of home.

I chose to go to Pure Wellness at Green Pastures because it is a church-based facility, and I thought that the trainers there would be more approachable for a physically disabled guy in his mid-thirties with little previous experience of exercise.

My initial hopes were fully realised. Pure and its staff quickly became hugely important to me, and they continue to hold a very special place in my heart today. The first time I walked into Pure, I was met by Gary Thompson, whom I had met several times over the years. I had called ahead so he was expecting me. As Gary chatted away, I glanced around at all the machines, most of which I had never seen before. The silver colouring on the Pure logo that adorned the wall convinced me that I had walked onboard a spaceship!

Gary took me round the equipment, patiently working out what I could and couldn't do. He was a massive help to me during my first few months in the gym. He always had time to move items around, lift down the lateral pulldown so that I could reach it, or make sure that my feet were properly secured into the rowing machine, as I couldn't manage this. He was and is a super guy. The same is true of another lad, Scott McGarry, who was on his way to becoming recognised as one of the best personal trainers in the UK, yet he never failed to notice if I needed a bench moved or a piece of apparatus adjusted, no matter how busy he was.

By the start of my second visit, Gary had devised a short exercise programme for me consisting of work on the lat pulldown, chest and shoulder press, and tricep rope then finishing off with light hand-held weights and basic crunches. I enjoyed this routine and worked at it diligently for months before the gym manager, Estelle Wallace, decided that it was time I moved up a gear in my training. 'I am going to book you an appointment with Aaron, another one of our personal trainers. He will help you to learn more exercises and you will see better results,' she said.

The following Thursday, I had what turned out to be the first of many sessions with Aaron Benton, who would have a massive impact on my life and my fitness over the next couple of years. Within a couple of weeks, I was doing supersets consisting of four different exercises with the weights, not to mention sit-ups, compound rows, and squats, while using the Smith Machine as a balancing aid.

Aaron became a great friend. We regularly took hair-raising spins in his car or went surfing at Portrush. Well, to be more precise, Aaron surfed while I sat on the beach, too scared to enter the water. We also prayed together about things that concerned me. Rachael and I were delighted to attend his wedding to Victoria around a year before ours, and Aaron was one of my groomsmen.

Back in the gym, we accomplished many challenges together. Arguably the most significant one being a 26.2-mile row-a-thon, which took place after months of arduous training, three mornings a week beginning at 7 a.m. I had told Aaron about my desire to set a goal to both improve my fitness and raise some funds for our favourite charities. Completing a conventional marathon was not possible for me because of the stress and potential long-term damage to my knees, ankles and feet. I thoroughly enjoyed rowing on the machine, so we decided that making the distance on that would be something to work towards.

So began the hard slog: weeks and weeks of bench presses, along with shoulder, arm, and chest work to build my upper-body strength. I did step-ups and extra squats to improve my leg power. Of course, all of these had to be combined with miles and miles of practice on the rowing machine. At one point, I was completing half-marathons before work. Even during the rigours of Spark week, I continued training, rowing a mere forty-seven kilometres in a five-day period between 7 a.m. and 9.30 a.m., after which I left the gym to take charge of thirty eager teenagers.

Originally, the row-a-thon was planned for August 2013 but was postponed due to the sudden death of a member of the Executive Team at Green Pastures. Thirty-two-year-old Russell Cairns died in a traffic accident the day before my event was to be held. Quite rightly, the gym closed in the week leading up to Russell's funeral.

I had known Russell for many years. He undertook his work experience from school at the *Ballymena Times* and later became a key figure in the launch of several effective social outreaches in Ballymena, including the foundation of Pure Wellness gym, where so many people have been introduced to the Lord Jesus. He was a lovely guy who made a wide mark in his short life.

I eventually put on my trainers to set my distance challenge at 9 a.m. Tuesday, 13 October that year. I planned to split the proceeds between the Cedar Foundation, which had helped me so much in early adulthood, and the Make-A-Wish Foundation. I selected this charity because it had sent my Aaron to Disney World in Florida when he developed cancer in his leg as a teenager. Representatives from both organisations visited the gym to 'wave me off' in the metaphorical sense. The marathon was divided into five segments of eight and a half kilometres each.

At the end of each segment, I could step off the rowing machine for a protein shake and a brief stretch to prevent my body from going into spasm. Each break could last only round five minutes. Any longer and my muscles would enter recovery mode, which I had to avoid before the row-a-thon was finished.

The first segment passed reasonably easy. I was in the excited 'Look at me; I am doing a marathon' mind-set. By the beginning of the third segment, my muscles were stiffening, and I feared I would have to stop. But Rachael, bless her, remained at my side for virtually the whole day and whispered words of encouragement that kept me going.

Rachael drew the line at granting a request to rub my bottom, which was aching at the close of the fourth segment. After over four hours on the rower, my backside felt like it had been sitting on a pointed rock. The dubious honour of massaging my rump fell to Aunt Mary, who tended to my needs while my mother, Rachael, and personal trainer giggled hysterically.

With my bum intact, I completed the final leg of my 'race'—the last leg feeling quite like the first in the sense that I was feeling upbeat about what I was doing, and I knew I was on the verge of accomplishing something big.

My overall finishing time was five hours and fourteen minutes. I was chuffed when Aaron described my efforts as 'an incredible feat' on social media and even happier that I had made my darling Rachael proud of me. After reaching the 'finishing post', I headed off to a hot bath followed by an Alison Moyet concert, happy in the knowledge that I had raised £1,000 for two super charities.

Soon afterwards, Aaron treated me to curry at a nearby Indian restaurant where he asked if I would be interested in serving in Pure Gym as a volunteer for a few hours a week. My job would be to answer the telephone and make sure the members signed in as they entered the premises.

This opportunity excited me as I loved Pure and the people who worked and trained there. It provided me with an interest outside of my writing, my relationship, and my home, something that was important for my self-esteem. I enjoyed getting up to mischief with Aaron before he moved on and now it is my privilege to work alongside the team there as we show the love of God to others through fitness. I consider it a joy to pray with and talk to people as they go in and out each morning. I have been blessed to be part of some genuine God moments, often with the most unlikely of people, and I hope I have made and will continue to make a difference in the kingdom of God through my service there.

CHAPTER TWENTY-SIX

'WOULD YOU LIKE TO DO SOME WRITING FOR US?'

A New Place of Work

Although I still enjoyed writing for the *Ballymena Times*, by October 2015 the organisation had changed beyond recognition from the Morton Newspaper group I had joined eighteen years earlier. Much more emphasis was now being placed on securing advertising. Despite our fantastic churches and community coverage, not to mention some excellent work from our own advertising team, an increasing number of churches switched their advertising to our larger, more widely read opposition paper.

Consequently, I the column inches dedicated to religious news in our newssheet was reduced considerably. Freelance payments were also taking longer to come through. Although the local office staff of the *Ballymena Times* always welcomed me, the company managers at the highest echelons were unable or unwilling to pay for freelance writers.

I sensed that my days at the *Ballymena Times* were numbered. However, because the paper had been part of my life for so long, when the axe came, it was still a shock, akin to a bereavement.

I had just conducted an interview with a missionary whose office was close to my home. When he left, I logged on to my work emails to find a message from Dessie asking me to ring him when I was free. Immediately, I sensed in my heart what was about to happen. I even said to Rachael, 'I think I have just done one of the final interviews for the *Ballymena Times*.'

I rang Dessie after lunch. Ever the gentleman, he gave me the news as honestly and compassionately as was possible under the circumstances. 'Son, head office is trying to save money whatever way they can. I have just taken a phone call telling me to cut all freelance cover with immediate effect. What this means is that they won't be paying for anymore freelance writing after thirty-one October.'

'Okay, Des.' I understood in my head what he was saying without applying it to my heart. 'If you need a hand with anything church-related, give me a call. I am happy with a by-line.'

I think it was after I put the phone down that the reality hit me. I walked silently into the living room where Rachael was sitting.

'Well, is your job gone?' she asked, giving me the opportunity for a simple response.

Unable to speak, I simply nodded and sat down, without any idea what my next occupational move might be. I also rang Mum, who was sympathetic but reminded me that the news was hardly unexpected given the current economic climate.

However valid the reasons for letting me go were, they didn't change the fact was also newly married, and every penny, even the small amount allowed under the permitted work scheme was important. I needed to find other work and quickly. Psychologically, I knew I would struggle to be content with anything outside the journalistic sphere, for it was everything I had known since I was eighteen years of age and the only form of work that had ever brought me lasting satisfaction. I enjoyed volunteering at Pure, but reporting was my passion and a reason to get up in the morning. At only thirty-eight, I had more to give in this field.

With this mind-set, my first move was to email the editor of the *Ballymena Guardian* to offer my services as a freelance Church News writer. I did not receive any response. Hardly surprising, given that I had worked for the opposing news rag for nearly two decades. My hasty communication also overlooked the fact that the *Guardian* had also made several cuts in recent years, so the chances of them having money to employ a new freelancer were non-existent, even at the tiny permitted work rates.

Out of courtesy to those whom I had written for during my newspaper years, I sent an email to all my contacts informing them that I was no longer working for the *Ballymena Times.* This letter unintentionally led to a few doors opening for me to keep writing. These opportunities included a request from Reaching & Teaching Ministries, a Ballymena-based charity Kenneth Wilson had set up to show God's love in practical and spiritual ways to people in the Philippines. Kenneth very kindly asked me to contribute to his ministry's twentieth anniversary booklet. This involved compiling longer articles than had been possible at the newspaper and was God's way of training me for what was to come.

Gordon Montgomery, co-owner of MCC Computers, a long-standing business in the town, heard that I had left the *Ballymena Times.* Together with his business partners, Philip and Sylvia McCartney, he had set up and funded an online project called www.thechurchpage.com, a site intended to give churches across the province an opportunity to freely share information, news, and event details.

Hearing of my availability, Philip rang me, and we arranged a meeting with Gordon to talk about The Church Page project to determine if I could help in some way. Predictably, I was extremely nervous in the run up to this meeting. At least ten years had passed since my last real job interview. Would they like me? Would I have anything to contribute to their website? This was a big opportunity to keep writing and probably one of the few roles I could realistically occupy.

My interview with Philip and Gordon was the toughest I have ever undertaken. Both men were pleasant to me throughout, but I found it difficult because they asked me about some of the problems I had encountered writing for and about churches over the years. I took the chance to spill my guts about the issues that had given my grey hairs for nearly two decades. I ranted about how churches had often been suspicious of my motives for contacting them and, therefore, had failed to engage with me.

Another issue was the inability of many fellowships to understand the importance of deadlines. I told them that I had lost count of the number of times a church representative had contacted me after the weekly submission date had passed with a request to promote an event just three days away.

Finally, I remarked that in my experience, Christian churches contained some of the least friendly, most sharp-tongued people I had encountered in twenty years of reporting. Many of those charged with contacting the press had poor people skills and seemed to delight in ripping the head off a poor local journalist who simply rang with the honest intention of promoting their congregations' events.

Knowing that I had read The Church Page, my potential employers canvassed my opinion on the site as it stood. I told that that it was an excellent concept, the site was well-designed and had huge potential. However, more content on the platform itself was needed to make the project more appealing to a wider audience.

I stated my belief that if news items were uploaded on a regular basis, people would be motivated to check it often to find material of interest to them. I told Philip and Gordon that I could quickly increase the volume of articles on their domain, which would, in turn, lead to more people viewing the site. Additionally, I predicted that, given the number of churches in the province, if the concept of The Church Page caught fire, it could rival any publication in the country as *the* information source for people in interested Christian matters.

However, perhaps because of my earlier negativity, Philip and Gordon were noncommittal at the end of the meeting about whether I would get the chance to work for them. They did promise to speak to the rest of the team and get back to me one way or another. I left their office and returned to Pure, which was next door. Seeing the tension on my face, Estelle Wallace kindly donned her boxing pads and allowed me to beat out my anxiety.

I was visiting my parents the following Monday when the phone rang. To my relief it was Philip McCartney inviting me to return to the office to arrange a start date to begin writing on The Church Page website. At the second meeting, which took place a couple of days later, I was introduced to Ally

Stewart, with whom I would be working directly on the project. She planned for me to begin my new role on 15 November 2015.

I was back! I recognised it then and still do today that this opportunity was a miracle only God could have performed. I had been let go by the newspaper when other publications were not hiring. Several other journalists with a higher profile and much more talent than I did were unable to find work in the field. But this door had opened in just a couple of weeks. Only God could have worked this out and I praise Him to this day for how He allows me to do the job I love.

My first piece for The Church Page went live on 17 November 2015. It was my introduction to the readers, letting them know that I had joined the team here from the *Ballymena Times*. It worked brilliantly as a means of letting church and Christian organisations know exactly where I was. Soon we had pieces coming in from The Faith Mission, Belfast City Mission, and other groups for which I had written regularly over the years.

The success of these pieces and the ones I continue to write is in no small measure due to the work of my colleague Ally Stewart, who works tirelessly on The Church Page and other MCC sites to ensure that key words and phrases from the blogs are optimised in order to reach the widest possible audience. Ally is an excellent blogger in his own right, and his work has played a central role in making our site the province-wide news source it is today.

I received a text from Ally a month or so after my arrival at The Church Page telling me that a blog we had published on The Francine Foundation, a Christian charity in India, was performing better on Google than a similar article published at the same time by my former employers. Upon receiving this text, I experienced momentary mixed emotions. I bore no hard feelings towards the *Ballymena Times* or anyone there. I had been part of their team virtually since boyhood and I wished them well. That said, I was proud to have become part of The Church Page and do the job for them I knew I was up for. No room for sentimentality.

Since that time, The Church Page has gone from strength to strength. The website regularly gets around 180 views per day compared with seventeen per day in 2014. The number of people accessing our blog through Facebook usually add around 6,000 to 10,000 per week to that number and sometimes more. Our Twitter feed receives around 6,000 impressions in a twenty-eight-day period. We do not pay for any of these; all our readership figures are organic.

Churches from County Antrim to County Armagh and everywhere in between contact us each week asking for their stories to be published. Ally and I publish up to three times a day during the week and sometimes on weekends.

Our most widely read story to date is 'An Appreciation of the Life of Archdeacon Kevin

Donnelly', who served for many years in the Parish of Kirkinriola, which includes Ballymena. Over 14,000 people read through our Facebook page news of his passing in September 2016. It is a real privilege to highlight charitable appeals made by churches and missionary organisations seeking finances, materials, or equipment.

We are encouraged to hear that people have given to a project after they have 'read about it on The Church Page.' While it is important to stress that everything good is provided by our generous and merciful God, it is a great blessing to know that He allows people like us help to build his kingdom.

CHAPTER TWENTY-SEVEN

'WE WANT TO READ YOUR STORY'

The Place Where I Always Wanted to Be

Older and wiser Christians have often told me, 'God never takes something away from you without replacing it with a blessing that is better.'

God opened the floodgates to yet more blessing when He allowed me to compile 'A Celebration of God's Kitchen', a small book detailing the history of a Luncheon Club for senior citizens run at my spiritual home, Kells Presbyterian Church.

Mum was the original head cook at the outreach, which celebrated its thirtieth birthday in 2017. She recently returned to the club as a helper and was delighted when I suggested writing a book to mark three decades of hot meals from God's own scullery in Kells, the village acknowledged as the birthplace of the 1859 evangelical revival that swept through Northern Ireland and saw 100,000 people give their lives to Christ.

Rev Brian and Robin Fowler, current chairperson of the group, welcomed my idea to create a miscellany of member contributions, poems, and details of the Luncheon Club's history. Robin quickly set about securing materials and sponsorships for the book. Anyone would have been proud to participate in this wonderful, eighty-page colour volume of rich memories. We printed and sold 300 copies, with the profits going towards club funds and the Flight for Flight charity, founded by Kat Duncan, a young missionary who grew up in Kells and works tirelessly to end the wicked practice of child trafficking on the streets of Sao Paulo.

Putting together the book gave me an opportunity to return to the fellowship I grew up in—the place where I called home and loved with all my heart. Having exited so quickly on the Sunday before my wedding, it was wonderful to go back for a brief time and say thank you to treasured friends, leaving the volume as a parting gift.

Since then, God's hand has remained on my career both at The Church Page and as a freelance writer. The idea for this *Trading Places* emerged during a conversation with Alistair Bates in his capacity as chair of the Author's Panel at Timeless Publications.

I had helped to write a script for someone else and passed it to him for consideration. As we talked, he said, 'Joe, as I read this, my thought was that the story I really want to read is yours.'

Flattered, I was unsure if anyone would be interested enough to read a book about me. Then Alistair said that the publisher was running a series on how God had changed the lives of individual Christians. He intimated that how I had gone from a premature, handicapped baby with an uncertain future to a married, graduate journalist would inspire others.

I promised to switch on my laptop, start typing and if anything meaningful appeared on the screen, I would let him know. What you are reading is a result of that promise and of the strength God gave me to write it. I could not have written ten words without His help, much less 40,000. To God be the glory and the increase.

CHAPTER TWENTY-EIGHT

'NOW IT ALL MAKES SENSE'

Postscript

At the beginning of this book, I set out with three objectives:

To reveal how God has worked in my life—a very ordinary one— and altering the course of my existence for the better

To show how God has been with me on a journey of grace, shaping every step of my life for His glory, for my good, and for the good of others

To tell you how God moved generously and miraculously to fulfil my dream of becoming a journalist, even when the world said it was impossible

Through the key details of my family background, birth and subsequent bleak prognosis, I have demonstrated that only for the direct intervention of God, my life would be, at best, very different and, at worst, non-existent. Remember, the doctors couldn't tell our parents whether Mark and I would survive. God ensured that we would. The paediatricians who labelled me 'retarded' at just under two years old and then 'slow to learn' at fourteen were both experts in their fields. I do not believe that both could have been so profoundly wrong. I praise God for rewriting my destiny and for sending me to university, to work, and into a loving marriage.

Secondly, I pray that by opening my heart to you about how I fell away from God, nearly losing my sanity and my relationships before He in His grace and mercy restored everything, you grasp that no one is beyond His reach. It doesn't matter how badly you have messed up or how or to what levels that person you love and pray for has failed, there is always a way to God, to meet Him for the first time or to renew your relationship with Him. His grace is restorative and perfect.

My aspiration is that you understand that God's grace for living not only 'saved' me from hell but also honoured His name my improving my life-chances as well as others in similar positions. My God-story shows that He has no favourites. Even when the world says you are too disabled or weak to make a difference, God can intervene to change the script.

Armed with the knowledge that the Lord governs every step His child takes, I can now see why God allowed me to go through that tough time at secondary school and why the doctor was permitted to say that my intelligence was 'below normal'. He needed someone with the courage to go to the people at the top and force them to change their practices. The person God chose for this was me. I experienced rejection and knew what it was to feel underestimated; however, the Lord also gave me the drive to get back up again. The same God who cares for two sparrows used me to ensure that never again will a young disabled person go to the North-East Institute or any other college and be dismissed without thought.

He also allowed me to look on as He ensured those with cerebral palsy or any other type of brain injury need not be robbed of a qualification because of their brain chemistry under pressure. God sent me to challenge people who run special schools or training programmes for disabled people. The Lord who created everyone in His image used me as a vessel to challenge the earthly decision makers who would impose a 'one size fits all' strategy and expect the service user to either fit in or lump it. Young people, disabled people, and indeed anyone who may have made mistakes or been impacted by adverse circumstances can attain their hearts' desires if they walk with God. I pray that my life has graciously shown what is possible with God.

Finally, my God-inspired journey from failing office trainee to province-wide journalist and author came via a route only God could plan, from interviewing NICOD trainees about their experiences at a training centre to questioning a future UK Prime Minister,

David Cameron, not to mention thousands of Christian articles and several books. What an amazing God! No words of praise I could never utter will be enough to express my thanks. The words of a little chorus I sang in Sunday school are running through my mind right now: 'Only Jesus, only Jesus, only He has done this' ('Sing to God', author unknown).

I give God all the glory for what He has allowed me to do and achieve. He makes no mistakes and has been in control of my every step. Every person I have ever met and each experience He permitted or organised for his purposes and glory. His Word says that His strength has been made perfect in my weakness (2 Corinthians 12:9). He created me for good works that he has prepared for me to do (Ephesians 2:10). Admittedly, there were times when I have not seen His hand on my life, nor have I always appreciated being 'refined' in His fire (1 Peter 1:7). However, the Lord has always revealed His purposes for all things to me, and time after time, He has acted for my good and His glory (Romans 8:28). What a God!

As a child, I didn't fully understand the first question and answer of the Westminster Shorter Catechism. By God's grace and mercy I understand them now and praise Him:

What is man's chief end?

Man's chief end is to glorify God and enjoy him forever.

God has been active in my life, even before I took my first breath, simply because He loves me. He has allowed me to enjoy the best possible existence on earth with a future address in heaven included as standard. I am forever thankful.

Acknowledgements

Indulge me for a paragraph or two longer as I pay tribute to the staff at NICOD/the Cedar Foundation, who were very supportive of me nearly two decades ago. I was a shy, vulnerable kid with big dreams but little idea of how to fulfil them. No doubt, I must have seemed like a mouthy little rebel without a clue as I failed to settle down to training in IT and Administration. They could easily have disregarded me as someone who didn't fit into their programmes and, therefore, didn't deserve to be there, but they modified what was on offer to give me a shot at achieving my ambitions. Bernie Graffin, Robert Wilson, Andrea McCaw, Anne-Marie McNulty, Elaine Armstrong, Shauna Smyth, Colin Robinson, Liz McKelvey, and Andrew Cooke, I honour you for your part in God's work to bring to where I am today.

I also want to thank Alistair Bates and the team at Timeless Publications for the opportunity to write this book and see it published. Erin Brown, who patiently edited the ramblings of a tabloid newspaper writer into a meaningful book, also deserves my unreserved gratitude. Thanks also to Roz Bowyer, my proof-reader who works alongside me on many of my freelance projects.

The same is true of my friend and colleague, Ally Stewart, who kindly masterminded the photographs that enliven this manuscript. Thanks also to Susan Pearson, who filled in the gaps that my mind had omitted from our physiotherapy sessions all those years ago.

I am honoured that Brian Boyd agreed to pen the foreword. I also thank Mum, Dad, Mark and Megan, and other family members for being part of the story. To my beautiful wife, Rachael, who too often heard 'just ten more minutes and I will be finished' over the past few months, thank you, darling, and I love you.

Most importantly, I once again thank God for making my impossible dream reality. I praise His risen Son, Jesus Christ, for saving me and being with me even though I have wondered from them at times. This story is a testament to their unfathomable love and patience.